ST MARY'S SCHOOL ASCOT

The Subject Leader's Handbook

Ian Nelson

Folens
Framework

Acknowledgements

The author is grateful to the Teacher Training Agency for permission to reproduce material from *National Standards for Subject Leaders* (1998).

Editor: Karen Westall   Layout artist: Patricia Hollingsworth
Illustrations: Trevor Green   Cover design: Martin Cross
Cover image: *Custer's Last Fight*, Unknown

© 1999 Folens Limited, on behalf of the author.

British Library Cataloguing in Publication Data. A catalogue record for this book is available from the British Library.

First published 1999 by Folens Limited, Dunstable and Dublin.
Folens Limited, Albert House, Apex Business Centre, Boscombe Road, Dunstable, LU5 4RL, England.

ISBN 1 85008 171–9

Printed in Singapore by Craft Print.

Contents

Introduction

The subject leader has a central role in promoting high standards within our schools. The importance of this leadership role is recognised by the significance placed on it during inspections and by the publication of the national standards for subject leaders by the Teacher Training Agency.

Aims of the book

This book is intended to offer practical advice and guidance on the roles and responsibilities of the effective subject leader. It is aimed at those aspiring to subject leadership posts as well as those currently holding those positions. It gives you the opportunity to evaluate your current performance and to identify ways of improving it. It will help to familiarise you with the national standards before exploring ways of establishing the current state of your subject, and how to raise standards by devising, implementing and monitoring a subject development plan.

Contents of the book

Chapters 1–4 give you the opportunity to evaluate yourself against the national standards. We are grateful to the Teacher Training Agency for permission to reproduce extracts from the standards within this book for this purpose. We must emphasise, however, that the exercises based on the standards are not part of the standards themselves and are not a requirement of the Teacher Training Agency.

Having familiarised yourself with the standards and with your current strengths and weaknesses as a subject leader, the book goes on in Chapter 5 to give practical suggestions for undertaking a comprehensive subject audit. This enables you to get a clear picture of your subject and its current strengths and areas in need of development. In Chapters 6 and 7, the book guides you through the creation, implementation and monitoring of a subject development plan based upon your subject audit.

The book recognises that you will raise standards through effective leadership and management of your team. It offers clear practical tips on how to improve your leadership and management techniques and includes a recommended reading list for those who wish to explore the theory of leadership and management in more depth.

Chapter

1

Subject leadership – the national standards

The national standards for subject leaders

Increasingly, teachers are expected to take on the role of subject leader within their school. This is a vital role and, if undertaken effectively, can have a significant impact upon the quality of education and standards of attainment within the school. Some schools, however, still define the subject leader's role in terms of day-to-day administrative tasks rather than in terms of the strategic development of the subject. The subject leader's job description might include a strategic development role. However, subject leaders are sometimes only expected to organise resources and to look at teachers' weekly planning. They are expected to draw up policies and schemes but are less likely to have done a comprehensive audit of their subject and set long term targets which impact upon all staff.

While subject leaders are generally expert within their own subject and confident and competent within their own teaching, often they have had little professional development in the management skills required to be an effective leader. The national standards for subject leaders are divided into five parts:

1. Core purpose of the subject leader.
2. Key outcomes of subject leadership.
3. Professional knowledge and understanding.
4. Skills and attributes.
5. Key areas of subject leadership.

Exercise

1. Write down in a single sentence what you think the core purpose of subject leadership is.

_____

_____

_____

2. Write down briefly what you think the key outcomes of subject leadership are.

_____

_____

_____

_____

_____

continued

3. Write down what you see as the professional knowledge and understanding needed for effective subject leadership.

_____

_____

_____

_____

_____

_____

_____

4. Write down what you see as the skills and attributes needed for effective subject leadership.

_____

_____

_____

_____

_____

_____

_____

_____

_____

5. Write down what you think are the key areas of subject leadership.

_____

_____

_____

_____

_____

_____

_____

_____

The national standards run to 12 pages so we cannot print the whole text here and you would be well advised to secure a copy of your own from the Teacher Training Agency. We can summarise the contents briefly under each of the headings and you can check to see how closely your understanding of subject leadership matches that laid down in the standards. We will look at each area in more detail in later chapters.

1. Core purpose of the subject leader

Under the core purpose of subject leadership, the emphasis is firmly on improved standards of attainment. The standards state as the core purpose:

> 'To provide professional leadership and management for a subject to secure high quality teaching, effective use of resources and improved standards of learning and achievement for all pupils.'

The whole reason for having subject leaders is to ensure high quality provision which raises the standards of attainment of all pupils. The emphasis throughout this book will be on your role as subject leader impacting positively upon standards of attainment.

2. Key outcomes of subject leadership

The key outcomes of effective subject leadership are detailed in the standards in terms of its impact on various groups of people within school. Effective subject leadership results in:
– pupils who show sustained improvement in the subject
– teachers who work well as a team, have secure subject knowledge and set high expectations for their pupils
– parents who are well informed and supportive
– headteachers and senior managers who understand the needs of the subject so that they can make informed decisions
– other adults in the school who are well informed and enabled to play an effective role in the delivery of the subject.

3. Professional knowledge and understanding

This includes subject-specific and generic knowledge and understanding. It includes an understanding of:
– the school's aims, priorities, targets and action plans
– the relationship of the subject to the curriculum as a whole
– any statutory requirements
– the characteristics of high quality teaching
– how research and inspection evidence can be used
– how to use comparative data to set targets for improvement
– how to develop literacy, numeracy and IT skills through the subject
– how teaching the subject can promote pupils' spiritual, moral, social, cultural, mental and physical development
– management including employment law, personnel, change, equal opportunities and finance
– how teaching can prepare pupils for adult life
– the potential of information technology for aiding teaching and learning in the subject
– school governance
– the implications of information and guidance from government departments and national bodies
– the implications of the Code of Practice for special educational needs
– health and safety requirements.

4. Skills and attributes

Subject leaders require a wide range of skills which come under the four broad headings of:
- leadership
- decision-making
- communication
- self-management.

In addition, they should possess a number of attributes or personal qualities.

5. Key areas of subject leadership

The standards identify four key areas of subject leadership and provide a great deal of detail about what subject leaders should be doing under each. The four areas are:
- strategic direction and development of the subject
- teaching and learning
- leading and managing staff
- effective and efficient deployment of staff and resources.

And you thought you were just a teacher!

The way forward

So how does your understanding of subject leadership compare with that outlined in the national standards? You might already be identifying areas of strength and areas where you feel less confident. You might also find that your subject leader job description does not include all the points outlined in the standards. This is an issue for the school's senior management team to address if it is to make the most effective use of its subject leaders and it may provide your next opportunity to practise your communication skills!

We will focus in future chapters on the areas outlined in the national standards, and you will be able to do some self-assessment exercises to help you to identify where you have strengths and where you might need to develop further to increase your effectiveness in your role as subject leader. Having looked at the national standards in some depth, we will relate these to the development cycle that will help you to ensure that your subject thrives and that pupils make effective progress in it. The cycle involves much the same as a well-produced business plan which outlines clearly:
- where you are now
- where you want to get to
- how you will get there
- how you will monitor progress towards your targets.

Future chapters

Having introduced the national standards, the next three chapters give more detail about them and allow you to evaluate your current performance as a subject leader. Chapter 2 looks at the core purpose and the outcomes of the standards, while Chapter 3 focuses on the skills and attributes of the subject leader. Chapter 4 considers the key areas of subject leadership. Once we have looked closely at the national standards, the later chapters give clear guidance on how to put the standards into practice by undertaking a comprehensive subject audit, and producing, implementing and monitoring a subject development plan.

Chapter 2

The core purpose and key outcomes of subject leadership

After a wide consultation with a variety of interested bodies, the TTA has defined the core purpose and the key outcomes of subject leadership. This chapter will give you the opportunity to assess how closely you achieve these through a series of self-evaluation exercises.

The core purpose

The core purpose of the subject leader is to provide professional leadership which secures good quality teaching and improved standards for all pupils. The following exercise enables you to check how effectively you think you achieve the core purpose at the moment. Score yourself on a four-point scale where 0 = not at all, 1 = insufficiently, 2 = satisfactorily and 3 = considerably.

A subject leader ...	Grade	Evidence to support the grade
provides leadership and direction		
provides management and organisation		
secures high standards of teaching and learning		
plays a major role in the development of policy and practice		
ensures that practices: – improve the quality of education provided – meet the needs and aspirations of all pupils – raise standards of achievement		
supports, guides and motivates teachers and other adults		
evaluates: – the effectiveness of teaching and learning – the subject curriculum – progress towards targets for staff and pupils		
monitors the subject		
identifies needs of his/her subject		
considers subject needs in relation to overall school needs		
understands how the subject contributes to school priorities		

One of the aspects of an external inspection is leadership and management and the team has to report on various issues within it. Clearly, your grades on this exercise might well be informed by your latest inspection report. Once you have read through this book and tried some of the ideas within it, you might like to repeat this questionnaire and see if you have improved your impact on the core purpose of your role. By the time you have undertaken the audits and devised, implemented and monitored your subject plan according to the guidance in this book, you should be scoring three consistently against each element of the core purpose.

The key outcomes of subject leadership

Subject leadership impacts upon pupils, teachers, parents, the head and senior staff and upon other adults, including administrative and support staff. This is an initial opportunity to assess how effectively you think you are achieving the key outcomes of your role as subject leader. In the case of the outcomes in relation to pupils and teachers, you will find clear guidance in Chapter 5 on undertaking comprehensive audits of standards, progress and teaching which will form the basis of your position statement and development plan.

At this stage, you are familiarising yourself with the national standards and doing simple checks based upon your current perceptions. The audits will give you a clearer idea of how accurate you have been in assessing your achievements here. Again, once you have completed the book and followed its suggestions you should be able to score three for each element of the key outcomes. Score on a four-point scale where 0 = no effect, 1 = insufficient, 2 = satisfactory and 3 = considerable.

The outcomes of effective leadership on pupils

Effective subject leadership results in pupils who ...	Grade	Evidence to support the grade
show sustained improvement in knowledge, understanding and skills		
understand the key ideas of the subject		
show improvement in literacy, numeracy and information technology skills		
know the purpose and sequence of activities		
are well prepared for tests and exams		
are enthusiastic about the subject		
contribute to a purposeful working environment through their attitudes and behaviour		

The outcomes of effective leadership on teachers

Effective subject leadership results in teachers who ...	Grade	Evidence to support the grade
work well together as a team		
support the aims of the subject		
know how the subject aims relate to the school aims		
are involved in the formation of policies and plans		
apply policies and plans consistently in the classroom		
are dedicated to improving standards of teaching and learning		
have an enthusiasm for the subject which motivates pupils		
have high expectations of pupils		
set pupils challenging but realistic targets based upon a good knowledge of the pupils and the progression of the concepts in the subject		
make good use of guidance training and support to enhance their knowledge and understanding of the subject and develop their expertise		
take account of relevant research and inspection findings		
make effective use of subject-specific resources		
select appropriate teaching and learning approaches to meet subject-specific objectives and the needs of all pupils		

These grades represent your initial views. Once you have worked through some of the ideas in this book, you might wish to review them. You should always be aware of the key outcomes of subject leadership and they should help to guide you towards using your time and that of others as effectively as possible to ensure constant improvements to standards. The next sections of the key outcomes refer to their impact upon parents, the head and senior managers and other adults involved in the subject. After each, there is some guidance on how you might check your perceptions against those of the other parties involved and improve your performance.

The outcomes of effective leadership on parents

Effective subject leadership results in parents who ...	Grade	Evidence to support the grade
are well informed about their child's achievements and targets for further improvement		
know the expectations made of their child in learning the subject		
know how they can assist and support their child's learning		

Reports to parents

There are three elements to this outcome. Firstly, do pupils' reports in your subject say quite clearly what each pupil:
– has achieved and
– needs to do next?
Do reports focus on what the pupils know, understand and can do as well as their attitudes to work? Are they written in language which is accessible to the lay person? Are they informative enough for those parents who can't or won't attend open evenings to discuss their child's work?

These are the kind of questions the effective subject leader needs to ask and it may be that you need to seek the answers from the parents themselves. After all, what is perfectly clear to you as a teacher and a subject leader might be totally unclear to those with a different perspective.

Clearly, if you are going to undertake a survey of parents' opinions on school reports, you need to liaise with other departments in doing so. You must be clear what you need to know from the parents, how you are going to find out and what you are going to do with the information they give you. If you are going to ask them to complete a written survey, check with other subject leaders and the senior management team so that such a survey can be well coordinated and cover all subjects. You might use the kind of grid shown on p. 13 to check opinions against subjects and include space for comments.

Parental survey on school reporting

We would like to know how we can improve our school reports and any other information which we give you about your child's work. It would help us if you could complete the following questionnaire. The subjects that we cover are listed down the side of the grid. Across the top are four statements about reports in each subject. For each subject that your child takes, please give a grade where 0 = not at all clear, 1 = a little unclear, 2 = clear enough, 3 = very clear.

Subjects	I am clear about what my child knows, understands and can do in this subject	I am clear about what my child needs to do to improve in this subject	I am clear about what is expected of my child in this subject	I am clear about how I can help my child to improve in this subject
English				
Maths				
Science				
Art				
etc.				

I would like to suggest the following ways to improve the information you give me about my child's work.

An alternative to a written survey would be to get each teacher to ask parents at open evenings for their views on the current reporting arrangements. However, this will only provide the views of those who attend and will lengthen the open evening considerably. A third alternative would be to hold an evening where parents could work in groups to voice opinions on current reporting arrangements and work with teachers on improving them. You can also refer to the relevant questions from the OFSTED parents' questionnaire.

Parental understanding

The second element in this section concerns whether parents understand the expectations made on their children in your subject. This involves your considering whether you give parents adequate information about what their children will be doing over each year, how they will be doing it and how they will be assessed. You need to check that the section on your subject in the school prospectus is up to date and adequately reflects the current work that pupils cover. You can also produce a separate subject-specific information sheet explaining in more detail the expectations of your subject on pupils in each year group. If you are going to do this, consider the possibility of involving parents in its production or at least in voicing their views in draft form.

Parental assistance Within this kind of document, you could include the third element from this section by offering clear guidance on how parents can help their children to improve their knowledge, understanding and skills in your subject. Perhaps, as well as including the pupils' targets on their reports, you could include a section for parents on how they can help their child to improve.

The outcomes of effective leadership on the headteacher and senior managers

Effective subject leadership results in headteachers and other senior managers who ...	Grade	Evidence to support the grade
understand the needs of the subject		
use information about achievements and development priorities in the subject in order to make well-informed decisions and to achieve greater improvements in the whole school's developments and its aims		

Communicating needs to your seniors This section relates to your communication networks with the head and the senior management team. Just how do you ensure that they know what your subject needs in order to raise standards further? Just as importantly, how do you best convey the messages to ensure a positive response? The old saying about 'it's not what you say, it's the way that you say it' does hold a lot of truth. You need to express your needs in a way which helps the head and senior managers to see the benefits to themselves as well as to you and your subject. This is a point we will return to when we look at the subject development plan in Chapter 7 and there is also some useful guidance on effective communication in Chapter 3 concerning the skills of the subject leader.

The second element in this section again focuses on communication. Do you provide the information the head and senior management team need in a way which makes it easy for them to make effective use of it? Again, this will be considered when looking at subject development planning.

The outcomes of effective leadership on other adults

Effective subject leadership results in other adults in the school and community who are ...	Grade	Evidence to support the grade
informed of subject achievements and priorities		
able, where appropriate, to play an effective role in the teaching and learning of the subject		

The other adults referred to in this section might include:
– technical staff
– administrative staff
– classroom assistants
– external agencies
– representatives of business and industry.

How and what to communicate to others

You need to decide what other adults need to know and the best way to inform them. Try to ensure that you communicate to each group in a way most appropriate to that group without being patronising. Ask yourself why each group needs the particular information you intend to convey and how they would best like to receive it. Be clear in the first place about the role of each of these groups in the effective teaching and learning of your subject.

This chapter has introduced the core purpose of the subject leader and the key outcomes of effective subject leadership. It has given you an opportunity to evaluate how effectively you think you achieve them at the moment. The next chapter will focus on the knowledge, understanding, skills and attributes of the subject leader.

Chapter 3

Knowledge, understanding, skills and attributes

There is an increasing recognition that being an effective subject leader requires a body of knowledge and certain skills. The TTA has listed these in the standards for subject leaders and the purpose of this chapter is to introduce them. You will have the opportunity to assess yourself against the requirements before looking in more detail at the knowledge, understanding and skills required by the effective subject leader.

Knowledge and understanding

To begin with, try grading yourself on what you consider your knowledge and understanding to be, using the following four-point scale:
- 0 for no knowledge and understanding
- 1 for insufficient
- 2 for satisfactory
- 3 for considerable.

As you complete the exercise, try to list on a sheet of paper some of the evidence to support your grades. What might you say to an interview panel to justify any grades 2 or 3?

Subject leaders should have knowledge and understanding of ...	Grade
their school's aims, priorities, targets and action plans	
the relationship of the subject to the curriculum as a whole	
any statutory curriculum requirements for the subject and the requirements for assessment, recording and reporting of pupils' attainment and progress	
the characteristics of high quality teaching in the subject and the main strategies for improving and sustaining high standards of teaching, learning and achievement for all pupils	
how evidence from relevant research and inspection evidence and local, national and international standards of achievement in the subject can be used to inform expectations, targets and teaching approaches	
how to use comparative data, together with information about pupils' prior attainment, to establish benchmarks and set targets for improvement	
how to develop pupils' literacy, numeracy and information technology skills through the subject	
how teaching the subject can promote pupils' spiritual, moral, social, cultural, mental and physical development	
management, including employment law, equal opportunities legislation, personnel, external relations, finance and change	

continued

how teaching the subject can help to prepare pupils for the opportunities, responsibilities and experiences of adult life	
the current use and future potential of information and communications technology to aid teaching and learning of the subject, and to assist with subject management	
the role of school governance and how it can contribute to the work of the subject leader	
the implications of information and guidance from LEAs, the DfEE, WOED and other national bodies and associations	
the implications of the Code of Practice for special educational needs for teaching and learning in their subject	
health and safety requirements, including where to obtain expert advice	

Completing this exercise should have highlighted where you think you have good knowledge and understanding and where you need to improve it. Look at the areas where you have scored 0 or 1. List each of these elements in the box below and then consider alongside how you might gain the knowledge you need.

Areas I need to improve on	How I might gain the knowledge I need

How to gain knowledge

In some cases, the knowledge you require is already available in school and you simply need to access it. This will be the case for the school's aims and priorities, for example. It may also be the case for most of the statutory requirements, and for information and guidance documents. Make sure that you are familiar with the relevant documents and know where to access the information you need.

Make effective use of the expertise around you. Ask the special needs coordinator for advice on how to ensure that pupils with SEN receive appropriate support in your subject. Ask the IT coordinator to suggest ways in which you can use technology to support learning in your subject. Find out about the roles and responsibilities of the school governors and how you can help them to fulfil those roles. Consider a system of subject link governors, where each governor takes a particular interest in a subject, reporting on it regularly at governors' meetings. Talk with the school health and safety representative about any issues relating to your subject. Improve your management knowledge with some relevant reading and seek the bursar's advice on budget management and handling financial information. Make sure you read the educational press and subject association newsletters to keep up to date with changes in education in general and in your subject in particular.

Some elements might not be so easily accessible within school and may require you to seek advice from other sources such as your LEA adviser or professional association. Identify which these are and how you can best access them. Look at your own professional development needs and plan your course attendance to address the areas where you need to improve your knowledge and understanding the most. Talk to other subject leaders within your school and from neighbouring ones and see if there are issues common to several of you where you could seek support as a group. Remember that having the knowledge is one thing but using and applying it is quite another. The national standards emphasise that 'subject leader expertise is demonstrated by the ability to apply this knowledge and understanding in each of the key areas of subject leadership.'

Skills needed for effective subject leadership

The skills needed for effective subject leadership come under four headings:
- Leadership.
- Communication.
- Decision-making.
- Self-management.

Each is a major aspect and the best we can hope to achieve here is to introduce some ideas and give some guidance. A useful starting point again is a self-assessment exercise. Using the same four-point scale that you used to assess your knowledge and understanding (p. 16), grade yourself on the level of each skill that you think you have.

Consider what evidence you might have to support your scores. How could you convince an interview panel that you have considerable skill in prioritising, planning and organising or in chairing meetings effectively? What have *you* (rather than we, the department, or the school) actually done to demonstrate those skills in school recently?

Remember 0 = no skill, 1 = insufficient skill, 2 = satisfactory skill and 3 = considerable skill.

Leadership skills. Subject leaders should be able to ...	Grade
secure commitment to a clear aim and direction for the subject from colleagues	
prioritise, plan and organise	
work as part of a team	
deal sensitively with people, recognise individual needs and take account of these in securing a consistent team approach to raising achievement in the subject	
acknowledge and utilise the experience, expertise and contributions of others	
set standards and provide a role model for pupils and other staff in the teaching and learning of the subject	
devolve responsibilities and delegate tasks as appropriate	
seek advice and support when necessary	
command credibility through the discharge of their duties and use their expertise to influence others in relation to their subject	
make informed use of research and inspection findings	
apply good practice to and from other subjects and areas	
Decision-making skills. Subject leaders should be able to ...	
judge when to make decisions, when to consult with others, and when to defer to the headteacher or senior managers	
analyse, understand and interpret relevant information and data	
think creatively and imaginatively to anticipate and solve problems and identify opportunities	
Communication skills. Subject leaders should be able to ...	
communicate effectively, orally and in writing, with the headteacher, other staff, pupils, parents, governors, external agencies and the wider community, including business and industry	
negotiate and consult effectively	
ensure good communication with, and between, staff who teach and support the subject	
chair meetings effectively	
Self-management. Subject leaders should be able to ...	
prioritise and manage their own time effectively, particularly in relation to balancing the demands made by teaching, subject management and involvement in school development	
achieve challenging professional goals	
take responsibility for their own professional development	

Attributes of the effective subject leader

As well as requiring these skills, the subject leader also needs certain attributes or personal qualities. These are largely the attributes displayed by any successful and effective teacher, so try grading yourself against each of them on the usual four-point scale.

Attributes	Grade
personal impact and presence	
adaptability to changing circumstances and new ideas	
energy, vigour and perseverance	
self-confidence	
enthusiasm	
intellectual ability	
reliability and integrity	
commitment	

Having completed these self-assessment exercises, you should have identified quite clearly where your strengths are and where you need to improve. Make the same kind of list that you made in considering your level of knowledge and understanding to help you to identify where your main priorities are in professional development. Given that entire books have been written on each aspect of the skills listed above, this chapter will, of necessity, provide only an overview.

Managing yourself

The core purpose of the subject leader is to improve standards of learning and achievement for all pupils. This is why you are in that role. You can begin to identify which of your tasks are most useful in enabling you to achieve the core purpose with the following exercise. On the grid on p. 21, list all the tasks that you do as part of your job. Then give each a grade according to how much impact it has on your core purpose of improving standards.

Use the same grading system, where 0 = no impact, 1 = little impact, 2 = satisfactory impact, 3 = considerable impact. Again, include evidence where you can.

Core purpose	Grade for impact	Evidence of impact (or lack of)
To improve standards of learning and achievement for all pupils, I ...	which has this level of impact on pupil achievement	because ...
teach pupils		
prepare lessons		
mark books		
write policies		
write schemes of work		
write letters		
answer letters		
tidy the classroom		
plan next term's work		
sharpen pencils		

You are likely to have a very long list! This exercise should help to illustrate how some of the tasks that you do have much more impact on the core purpose of the subject leader than others. These should take priority when time is short. If you find that some of the tasks which have least impact are being generated by other people, you need to tackle those people about them. It may be that they have never thought about the consequences of what they consider to be simple demands. By discussing the nature of some of the tasks which you regard as rather pointless, you may be able to reduce them, or alternatively you may be persuaded that they are more significant than you thought. It may even be that, in talking with colleagues, you reach agreement that some of the tasks serve no useful purpose and can be dropped altogether!

In managing yourself effectively, it is essential that you focus on those tasks which have the greatest impact on your core purpose however much you might enjoy some of the less significant ones. Clearly, there will always be some tasks that do not seem to have a major impact upon pupil achievement but which are required by law or by the senior management team. In this case, you need to consider delegating some of them.

Effective delegation

Delegation is simply giving someone else the authority and resources to do part of your job. Clearly, there are parts of your job which you could not delegate, such as appraising staff. However, there may be some routine tasks which you could delegate, possibly to non-teaching staff, to parent helpers and to pupils in some cases. In delegating, it is important to explain exactly what is to be done, how it is to be done and to provide sufficient support to ensure that it is done successfully. Gradually, you can withdraw the support as the delegate gains confidence and competence with the task.

Remember, however, that although you can delegate the responsibility, you can never delegate the accountability. If things go wrong, you are still to blame. The two advantages of delegation are that it saves you time by cutting down on routine tasks and that it provides professional development for the person you delegate to as long as it is done properly. Try listing some of the jobs that you do which could be given to others. This chart will help you.

Delegation

What I do now
What I could delegate
Who *could* do it
Why I *should* delegate it to her/him (what benefits will she/he get?)

Planning and organisation

Usually, people will have in their diaries all the meetings they have to attend and occasional reminders of things they must do. In between will be plenty of spaces when they are actually planning to do things which do not merit a diary entry with a time. This creates the impression that meetings are more important than any other work you do and that other tasks can be fitted in around them. We will deal with meetings later but now we will consider the effective use of your diary or planner.

You might well make a daily 'to do' list. Often this only includes important jobs like telephoning someone or making sure you get some new books from the stock cupboard for a particular lesson. The benefit of a complete 'to do' list is that it lists *everything* you have to do, even the routine and mundane jobs. Don't forget to include teaching classes! Once you have written your list, transpose it to your diary, giving each item an allotted time, both starting and finishing. In this way, you can see exactly where your time is going. When someone asks you if you can spare a minute, you can answer truthfully!

This system will also give a clear indication of how much you need to delegate. For example, do you actually need to do the photocopying or the mounting of pupils' work yourself or could someone else, a parent helper perhaps, be persuaded and trained to do it for you? Another advantage of having your diary filled out properly is that it prevents anyone hijacking what looks like free time. There are always colleagues who are less well organised than you are and they will ask you to fit in an unexpected meeting at short notice. With most diaries, this goes into a blank space even though you had mentally reserved that time for a particular job which then has to be postponed and done some other time. Remember to include a space for completing tomorrow's diary! Below is an example of what your diary might look like if you adopt this system.

Example of a daily plan

Date Feb. 28th

7.00	7.30 leave for school
8.00 preparing classroom	8.30 photocopying
9.00 teaching	9.30 teaching
10.00 teaching	10.30 playground duty
11.00 teaching	11.30 teaching
12.00 lunch/marking books	12.30 preparing lessons
1.00 teaching	1.30 teaching
2.00 teaching	2.30 coffee break, see ... about ...
3.00 teaching	3.30 see parent
4.00 mounting work	4.30 marking books
5.00 checking catalogues	5.30 writing out order
6.00 leave for home	6.30 eating!
7.00 leave for school	7.30 parents' meeting
8.00 parents' meeting	8.30 parents' meeting
9.00 leave for home	9.30 reading TES

Clearly, the actual entries will reflect your particular phase of education and role in school. This will mean that if you have the luxury of non-contact time, you will allocate tasks to it in your diary rather than hoping nothing will crop up to rob you of the opportunity to catch up on a few jobs. Try completing your own diary for tomorrow using this format. If possible, try to build in contingency time to cope with the inevitable unforeseen emergency.

Meetings

Meetings take up an enormous amount of time and, although people may moan about them, few ever consider the impact of particular meetings on the core purpose of improving standards. Try to list each of the meetings that you regularly call or attend and, using the same four-point scale, grade each according to its impact on pupils' learning, where 0 = no impact, 1 = little impact, 2 = satisfactory impact, 3 = considerable impact.

Meeting	Grade	Evidence

If you have meetings which appear to have no impact on pupils' learning, you need to consider why you have them at all. It may be that the people calling those meetings have a different perception of their importance and that either you have missed the significance or they have their priorities wrong. In planning a meeting, you need to begin by asking how your pupils will benefit from it. If they won't, you have to consider whether you need it or whether there is an alternative way of achieving your objectives. For example, a meeting to brief staff might well be useful but could you brief them as easily through a simple A4 sheet of notes? Alternatively, a meeting to plan the following term's work is likely to have a major impact on pupils' learning. Set clear objectives for any meeting you convene. Make sure that you express them in terms of what the meeting will have achieved. For example, 'by the end of the meeting, we will have agreed the dates and formats for the parents' consultation meetings for the year' is more precise than a staff meeting about parents' evenings.

Consider also who needs to attend the meeting. What benefits do each of the participants gain from it? What is each likely to contribute? Do they need to attend the whole meeting or just part of it? Make sure that you do not waste the time of colleagues by inviting them to meetings which they do not really need to attend. Try the following format for a forthcoming meeting.

Attendee	What she/he will contribute	What she/he will gain

The agenda

Having established the need for a meeting, you should prepare the agenda. Often this includes the start time of the meeting but not the finish time. Include both so that those attending can plan the rest of their day. The agenda often simply lists vague headings with little indication of who will lead each item and whether it is there for discussion, for a decision or for information only. Also, each item is usually untimed, so if people only need to attend for a couple of items, they have no idea when these will be and end up staying for the whole meeting. Try the following agenda format.

Meeting agenda

Meeting	Date Time Venue Purpose		Those attending	
Agenda item		**Item leader**	**Time needed**	**Discussion, decision or information**
1.				
2.				
3.				
4.				
5.				
Pre-meeting preparation, papers attached.				

The minutes

Increasingly, meetings in school are minuted. These often take the form of copious notes about who said what, who agreed and who disagreed. You need to ask yourself why you need minutes in the first place and what is the best form for them. If most meetings are about getting things done, most require action notes rather than extensive accounts of the debates, although there will be some exceptions like annual general meetings which have to abide by a written constitution. For most work meetings, a brief summary in a format like the one below will suffice.

Action notes

Meeting	Attendance	Date
Who	**Will do what**	**By when**
Date of next meeting	Venue	

Chairing meetings

Poor chairing of meetings is one of the most common reasons for their failing. There are key elements to chairing a meeting and the best chairpersons are good at most of them. Some less effective chairs fail in some of the elements, which reduces the impact of the whole meeting. The elements of effective chairing are listed in the table below so that you can consider how skilled you are at each one and where you need to develop. Grade yourself on the same four-point scale for your skill on each item, where 0 = no skill, 1 = insufficient skill, 2 = satisfactory skill and 3 = considerable skill.

How good are you at ...	Grade	Evidence
starting meetings on time?		
encouraging discussion?		
keeping to the agenda?		
clarifying views?		
drawing out the less confident?		
preventing people from dominating?		
summarising what has been agreed?		
maintaining a balance of views?		
ensuring expert advice is available?		
checking commitment to decisions?		
ending the meeting on time?		

For an independent view on your ability as a chairperson, get a colleague to complete the grid after one of your meetings! To improve your chairing skills, try noting how those who chair effective meetings do so, as well as noting the things to avoid when you attend a badly chaired meeting. Think through what most irritates you about the way people chair meetings and what you might be doing to irritate others.

Leading and managing others

In most schools, the subject leader will have to make effective use of a team in order to accomplish the core purpose of his or her role. Much research has been conducted into what makes an effective team and Dr Meredith Belbin's work at Henley and Cambridge gives a clear indication that you do not get the best teams simply by putting together the most technically accomplished individuals. He concluded that everyone has a particular team skill to offer and getting the right balance of these skills creates a successful team. He developed a list of eight essential team roles, later adding a ninth. A team of less than nine means that members cover more than one role each. Everyone has a preferred role and a secondary one. He also identified the allowable weakness inherent in each team role.

As subject leader, you are unlikely to be able to choose your entire team. In fact, some of your team will be leaders of other teams within the school. However, having some understanding of team roles will give you some insight into why people react in such different ways to the same situation or message. Having some idea of their preferred team role can help you to anticipate reactions and to frame messages for each member of the team in a way which most appeals to him or her.

Belbin's essential team roles

- Coordinator.
- Plant.
- Resources investigator.
- Shaper.
- Monitor-evaluator.
- Implementer.
- Completer.
- Team worker.

He later added the role of *specialist* to this original list.

You can probably begin to identify the preferred roles of some of your colleagues, and yourself, by looking at the characteristics of each role. These are given on p. 28. You might well find that some of the roles do not appear to be filled by your colleagues, but a psychometric profile on each would distinguish their primary and secondary team roles and often someone in a team will adopt the 'missing' role quite naturally during the course of a project.

By understanding a little about team roles, you should be able to understand why giving certain types of tasks to certain people can be hugely successful or an absolute disaster. You will also appreciate the potential for conflict within a well-balanced team. We tend to like people like ourselves and fail to appreciate the strengths of those who are different. The obvious danger of this is that leaders might well be tempted to recruit only people like themselves, leaving the team seriously unbalanced in terms of team roles. By understanding the strengths and weaknesses of each team role, you can help the individuals within your team to appreciate each other's contribution more.

Team roles

The coordinator

- natural chairperson
- mature and confident
- talks and listens well
- clarifies goals
- promotes decision-making
- quiet charisma

allowable weakness

- a touch manipulative

The plant

- the team's vital spark
- source of ideas
- creative
- imaginative
- unorthodox

allowable weaknesses

- a bit of a handful
- head in the clouds

The resources investigator

- a fixer
- extrovert
- amiable
- wealth of contacts
- explorer of opportunities

allowable weaknesses

- undisciplined
- short attention span

The shaper

- self-elected task leader
- dynamic
- outgoing
- highly strung
- argumentative
- seeks ways around obstacles

allowable weaknesses

- tendency to bully
- not always likeable

The monitor-evaluator

- strategic
- sober
- introvert
- discerning
- able to analyse data
- rarely wrong

allowable weakness

- an unexciting plod

The implementer

- the team's workhorse
- turns ideas into action
- gets on with the job
- logical
- loyal
- disciplined
- reliable
- conservative

allowable weakness

- can only adapt if told precisely why

The completer

- a worrier
- a stickler for detail, deadlines and schedules
- relentless follow-through
- chief catcher of errors and omissions

allowable weakness

- can't let go

The team worker

- counsellor
- conciliator
- mildly social
- perceptive
- accommodating
- aware of undercurrents
- promotes harmony

allowable weakness

- indecisive

The specialist

- source of rare knowledge
- single-minded
- loner
- self-starter
- dedicated
- occasional dazzling breakthrough

allowable weakness

- concentrates on a narrow front

Can you work out from the brief descriptions above what team roles you and each of your colleagues is likely to prefer? Try the following exercise, putting the team roles against the names and also including the evidence for your choice. Dare you share your thoughts with your colleagues and complete the exercise together?

Name	Team role	Evidence

There are implications for who you ask to do what and for the levels of support you might have to give people faced with particular tasks. For example, would you expect the resources investigator or plant to make a first-rate job of analysing assessment data and producing a detailed report for the governing body? Would you expect the monitor-evaluator to be first choice to establish effective links with the local community? Would you expect the shaper to be overjoyed at the prospect of tidying out your stock cupboard?

This is not to say that you must never give these types of people these jobs, but rather that they will require more support in doing them than the more obvious choices might. In other words, the effective leader knows each of the team thoroughly and adopts an appropriate leadership style for the individual and for the context.

Leadership styles

There is no one best leadership style. There have always been managers and leaders who pride themselves on being towards one end or the other of a scale from autocratic to democratic. The autocratic managers pride themselves on being totally task-orientated, getting the job done whatever the cost, while the democratic managers have a real concern for their teams. The really effective leader adopts the most appropriate style for the person and the context.

This is much the same as the really effective teacher. In class, you will sometimes direct pupils closely in a particular task. You will tell them exactly what to do, how to do it and stand over them while they complete the task to your explicit instructions. On other occasions, you will give them a task with brief instructions and expect them to complete it with a minimum of teacher support. In some classes, you will be directing very closely the work of some pupils while others engaged on the same task will be allowed to get on with much more independence.

The effective leader

Leadership is much the same. The effective leader knows which members of the team need to be directed on which tasks, which can have the task delegated to them completely and which need levels of support between those extremes. The effective leader gives each team member the right level of challenge and support to ensure that the task is done successfully and that the team member grows as a result of having completed it.

The model below illustrates three zones: the comfort zone, the stretch zone and the panic zone. People achieve most when they are appropriately stretched. If they only do what they have always done, they will not grow and develop new skills. On the other hand, if they are given tasks which drive them straight into the panic zone, making them feel unable to cope, the task is likely to be done poorly and the person will diminish as a result. The effective leader strives always to stretch the members of the team without overburdening them.

Comfort, stretch and panic zones

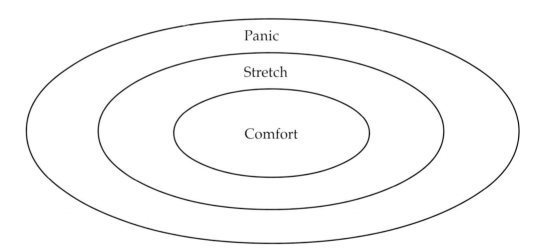

For example, one of your tasks as subject leader is to ensure the effective development of pupils' information technology skills through subject teaching. The teacher who regularly surfs the net will take offence at your explaining how to plug in the computer and insert the disk. On the other hand, the technophobic member of the department will panic if you suddenly require him or her to include in great detail in lesson plans exactly how IT skills will be used within lessons the following week. The first teacher will be frustrated at being kept firmly in the comfort zone, while the second will have gone straight into panic!

The effective leader might pair them up so that both are being stretched, one by being taught new skills and the other by having to teach them to a novice. In this way, one individual is directed so that he or she grows in confidence and competence in the use of IT while the other also benefits by being given responsibility for passing on his or her particular knowledge and expertise. You may well have a view of the current strengths and weaknesses of staff in terms of your subject and Chapter 5 will give you guidance on undertaking a formal audit of teaching to test the accuracy of those views.

Communication skills

Being a subject leader requires you to communicate effectively with a wide range of audiences. Before launching into any communication, you need to decide:
– what you want to communicate
– to whom you want to communicate it
– why you want to communicate it
– how to communicate for maximum impact.

Use the grid below to consider some of these issues.

Audience	What	Why	How
Headteacher	Subject development plan	To raise standards by improving resources	Written plan Short presentation to govs. and SMT
Other staff	How to use ICT in your subject	To increase staff confidence and raise standards in your subject and in ICT	Written guidelines Staff INSET
Pupils			
Parents			
Governors			
External agencies			
The wider community			

Keep a clear eye on your core purpose of raising standards of achievement in your subject. Ask yourself how this particular letter, report or presentation will impact upon standards. If it is not clear that it will, question whether it is needed at all. There is enough paperwork in school without your adding to it unnecessarily.

Focus your communication

Remember the WIIFM factor in any communication. This stands for What's In It For Me! Put yourself in the place of the receivers of your communication, either written or verbal, and ask why they should be interested in the first place. How often have you received junk mail and wondered why it was sent to you? Remember that some of your communications might be regarded in a similar light. Make them appeal to the specific audience by focusing on *their* interests and presenting them in a form which is easily accessible to *them*. Never assume that everyone else is as interested in every aspect of your work as you are.

Keep any communications you generate short and simple. It is much harder to produce a short report, letter or presentation than a long one but your audience will appreciate it. There is not space here to develop an entire effective communication skills course but it will be referred to again later in the book when we cover in some detail the specifics of your role, including the subject audit and subject development plan. Meanwhile, when you are producing written or oral communications, consider the following check-list.

Communications check-list

Key questions	Yes/No	Evidence
Am I clear what I want this communication to achieve?		
Am I aiming it at the right audience?		
Do I know what will influence this audience?		
Am I using the best medium for this message and this audience?		
Is the audience receiving the message I think I am sending?		
Is it clear to the recipients of the message what I want them to do with it?		

Decision-making

Effective decision-making is an essential attribute of the good leader in any walk of life. This involves gathering the information you need, consulting other interested parties, weighing up the alternatives and deciding on the best solution possible. It also involves thinking beyond the obvious and, at times, daring to be innovative. You can use the four Ps to help you to make decisions:

- Position.
- Possibilities.
- Problem.
- Proposal.

You begin by considering your present position. You will have a clear idea of what this is in your subject once you have undertaken the comprehensive subject audit outlined in Chapter 5, but, for the example here, imagine that you are on a journey and that your current *position* is Bath. The *problem* is that, having arrived at Bath, your car has broken down and you are due at a meeting in Bristol in an hour's time. The *possibilities* might be to wait for the breakdown service, to abandon your car and take a train, or to telephone your host and delay the meeting. Having drawn up your list of possibilities, you then need to gather any factual information, like train times, before coming to your *proposal* or decision. Clearly, if you have passengers, you may need to consult them at the possibilities stage and perhaps then 'sell' your decision to them. This mirrors the format for your subject audit and development plan where you need to know your current position, identify any problems arising from it, look at possible solutions and identify the best ones for your circumstances.

Communicating your decision

Having made a decision, you need to communicate it to all those who need to know. This would almost certainly include your team and may include also pupils, parents, senior managers and governors.

As subject leader, you will wish to involve your team in the decisions you have to make. This involvement will range across a spectrum similar to the autocratic to democratic one mentioned under leadership styles. In this case, there are five main points on the spectrum:

Telling   Selling   Testing   Consulting   Joining

At one extreme, you will tell the team after you have thought things through and decided the way forward. The team will conform to your decision. At the next stage, you sell the decision to the team, which involves your thinking things through and deciding the way forward before gaining the assent of the team. Beyond that is testing, where you think things through, propose possible solutions and make a decision. The team offers its views and gives agreement to the decision. Consulting involves presenting the problem to the team and seeking their ideas for solving it. You then make a decision. The team thinks things through and proposes ideas. The final stage is joining, where you and the team share control, with the team accepting responsibility for finding and implementing the solution. Your job as leader is to decide which of these stages is appropriate for which decisions.

In this chapter, we have looked at the knowledge, understanding and skills you need for effective subject leadership. Future chapters will build upon this brief overview and the list on p. 103 suggests titles for further reading on these issues. The next chapter looks at the key areas of subject leadership.

Chapter

4

The key areas of subject leadership

This chapter will introduce the key areas of subject leadership as laid down in the national standards. It will give you the opportunity to assess how well you think you are accomplishing the tasks and where you have room for improvement. There will also be an opportunity to compare your current job description with the tasks outlined in the key areas and to look at how you may need to amend it to reflect more fully the scope of the role and to match the standards.

The four key areas

A. Strategic direction and development of the subject
Within the context of the school's aims and policies, subject leaders develop and implement subject policies, plans, targets and practices.

B. Teaching and learning
Subject leaders secure and sustain effective teaching of the subject, evaluate the quality of teaching and standards of pupils' achievements and set targets for improvement.

C. Leading and managing staff
Subject leaders provide, to all those with involvement in the teaching or support of the subject, the support, challenge, information and development necessary to sustain motivation and secure improvement in teaching.

D. Efficient and effective deployment of staff and resources
Subject leaders identify appropriate resources for the subject and ensure that they are used efficiently, effectively and safely.

So how effectively do you achieve the tasks of the subject leader? In the following self-assessment exercise, try grading yourself against the tasks identified in the key areas. Use the same four-point scale where 0 = not at all, 1 = little achievement, 2 = satisfactory achievement, 3 = considerable achievement. Remember, as always, to list the evidence to support your grades. How would you justify your grades to an interview panel?

Self-assessment exercise

A. Strategic direction and development of the subject	Grade
A1. develop and implement policies and practices for the subject which reflect the school's commitment to high achievement, effective teaching and learning	
A2. create a climate which enables other staff to develop and maintain positive attitudes towards the subject and confidence in teaching it	
A3. establish a clear, shared understanding of the importance and role of the subject in contributing to pupils' spiritual, moral, cultural, mental and physical development, and in preparing pupils for the opportunities, responsibilities and experiences of adult life	
A4. use data effectively to identify pupils who are underachieving in the subject and, where necessary, create and implement effective plans of action to support those pupils	
A5. analyse and interpret national, local and school data, plus research and inspection evidence, to inform policies, practices, expectations, targets and teaching methods	
A6. establish, with the involvement of the relevant staff, short, medium and long term plans for the development and resourcing of the subject	
A7. monitor the progress made in achieving subject plans and targets, evaluate the effects on teaching and learning, and use this analysis to guide further improvement	
B. Teaching and learning	
B1. ensure curriculum coverage, continuity and progression in the subject for all pupils, including those of high ability and those with special educational or linguistic needs	
B2. ensure that teachers are clear about the teaching objectives in lessons, understand the sequence of teaching and learning in the subject, and communicate such information to pupils	
B3. provide guidance on the choice of appropriate teaching and learning methods to meet the needs of the subject and of different pupils	
B4. ensure effective development of pupils' literacy, numeracy and information technology skills through the subject	
B5. establish and implement clear policies and practices for assessing, recording and reporting on pupil achievement, and for using this information to recognise achievement and to assist pupils in setting targets for further improvement	
B6. ensure that information about pupils' achievements in previous classes and schools is used effectively to secure good progress in the subject	
B7. set expectations and targets for staff and pupils in relation to standards of pupil achievement and the quality of teaching; establish clear targets for pupil achievement, and evaluate progress and achievement in the subject by all pupils, including those with special educational and linguistic needs	
B8. evaluate the teaching of the subject in the school, use this analysis to identify effective practice and areas for improvement and take action to improve further the quality of teaching	

continued

B9. ensure effective development of pupils' individual and collaborative study skills necessary for them to become increasingly independent in their work and to complete tasks independently when out of school	
B10. ensure that teachers of the subject are aware of its contribution to pupils' understanding of the duties, opportunities, responsibilities and rights of citizens	
B11. ensure that teachers of the subject know how to recognise and deal with racial stereotyping	
B12. establish a partnership with parents to involve them in their child's learning of the subject, as well as providing information about curriculum, attainment, progress and targets	
B13. develop effective links with the local community, including business and industry, in order to extend the subject curriculum, enhance teaching and develop pupils' wider understanding	
C. Leading and managing staff	
C1. help staff to achieve constructive working relationships with pupils	
C2. establish clear expectations and constructive working relationships among staff involved with the subject, including through team working and mutual support; devolving responsibilities and delegating tasks, as appropriate; evaluating practice; and developing an acceptance of accountability	
C3. sustain their own motivation and that of other staff involved in the subject	
C4. appraise staff as required by the school policy and use the process to develop the personal and professional effectiveness of the appraisees	
C5. audit training needs of subject staff	
C6. lead professional development of subject staff through example and support, and coordinate the provision of high quality professional development by methods such as coaching, drawing on other sources of expertise as necessary	
C7. ensure that trainee and newly qualified teachers are appropriately trained, monitored, supported and assessed for the award of Qualified Teacher Status, the Career Entry Profiles and standards for induction	
C8. enable teachers to achieve expertise in their subject teaching	
C9. work with the SENCO and any other staff with SEN expertise to ensure that individual education plans are used to set subject-specific targets and match work well to pupils' needs	
C10. ensure that the headteacher, senior managers and governors are well informed about subject policies, plans and priorities, the success in meeting objectives and targets, and subject-related professional development plans	

continued

D. Efficient and effective deployment of staff and resources	
D1. establish staff and resource needs for the subject and advise the head and senior managers of likely priorities for expenditure, and allocate available subject resources with maximum efficiency to meet the objectives of the school, and achieve value for money	
D2. deploy, or advise the headteacher on the deployment of staff involved in the subject to ensure the best use of subject, technical and other expertise	
D3. ensure the effective and efficient management and organisation of learning resources, including information and communications technology	
D4. maintain existing resources and explore opportunities to develop or incorporate new resources from a wide range of sources inside and outside the school	
D5. use accommodation to create an effective and stimulating environment for the teaching and learning of the subject	
D6. ensure that there is a safe working and learning environment in which risks are properly assessed	

You will understand by now why the skills required for effective subject leadership introduced in the previous chapter include those of managing yourself, your time and other people effectively!

Your job description

Few subject leaders will have job descriptions which include this complete list of tasks in this format. It might be, however, that your current job description does include reference to many of them under broader headings. Try the following exercise to see how closely your job description matches the tasks of the key areas.

Using the grid on p. 38, write out the tasks listed in your subject leader's job description and tick which of the key areas each one applies to.

Matching your job description to the four key areas

Tasks from job description	Strategic direction and development of the subject	Teaching and learning	Leading and managing staff	Efficient and effective deployment of staff and resources
1.				
2.				
3.				
4.				
5.				
6.				
7.				
8.				
9.				
10.				
11.				
12.				
13.				
14.				

This exercise will reveal which of the key areas is under-represented in your job description. It will indicate whether your current role focuses too strongly on one or two areas to the detriment of the others. If you discover an imbalance, you may wish to discuss it with your headteacher. Before you do that, however, you might like to do a second, more detailed comparison to see which actual tasks from the key areas form part of your job description and which, if any, are missing.

Omitted tasks

In this exercise, you need to list the tasks from your job description along the top of the grid shown on p. 39 and the tasks from the key areas down the side. Then see if you can match them up. Although the language might differ between the key areas and your specified tasks, you are looking to see which of the key area tasks are already encompassed in your role.

When you have completed the grid, list the tasks from the key areas which are not part of your job description and also list any of your current tasks which do not feature in the key areas. This should give you a clear idea of how your job description may need to be modified to reflect fully the national standards. Any such modification will, of course, need to be negotiated with the headteacher and you may find that there are good reasons for any omissions or additions.

Matching job description to the key areas

Key areas/job tasks	1	2	3	4	5	6	7	8	9	10	11	12	13	14
A1 (see pp. 35–37)														
A2														
A3														
A4														
A5														
A6														
A7														
B1														
B2														
B3														
B4														
B5														
B6														
B7														
B8														
B9														
B10														
B11														
B12														
B13														
C1														
C2														
C3														
C4														
C5														
C6														
C7														
C8														
C9														
C10														
D1														
D2														
D3														
D4														
D5														
D6														

Tasks done by others   Clearly, the scope of your role as subject leader will depend upon a range of factors including:

– type of school
– size of school
– your experience and expertise.

In a large school, you might expect your job description to include most of the tasks covered by the key areas. In a smaller school, you might find your job description restricts you to policy development and looking after resources. If this is the case, you and the senior management team need to consider how the areas not included in your job description are actually covered in relation to your subject. It may be that the head alone does the monitoring of standards and quality, in which case you may need to negotiate tactfully for a stronger role with the support and training to go with it. It may be that the assessment coordinator does all the monitoring of standards achieved across the curriculum.

Having listed any of the tasks from the key areas that are not covered by your job description consider whether they are covered by other people.

Coverage of key areas

Tasks from the key areas not covered by my job description	Covered by headteacher	Covered by deputy head	Covered by assessment coordinator	Covered by SENCO	Covered by

You should now be very clear about which tasks from the key areas are not covered at all within the school and which are covered by people other than the subject leader. This is where you make full use of your negotiation and communication skills! You need to consult with your headteacher on both issues to ascertain why some of the key area tasks are not represented for your subject and why some are covered by other people. The reasons might include:

– pure oversight
– a lack of awareness of the national standards
– a desire to retain some aspects of the subject leader's role within the senior management team
– a perceived lack of experience or expertise on your part
– the fact that roles have always been allocated in this way
– a lack of clarity in job descriptions.

Of the tasks not already in your job description, which ones do you feel you could do successfully and which do you think you would need some support and training for? Draw up a list to show evidence of your ability to do those about which you feel confident and the support you feel you would need to do those about which you feel less confident.

Tasks which I could do	Evidence of my ability to do them	Tasks which I would need support with	Support required

Convincing others

If you wish to extend your current job description to match the key areas more closely, you now need to convince the head, senior management team and your colleagues of your ability to do so and of the benefits to them of letting you.

Remember the WIIFM factor from the communication skills section of the last chapter and focus on the benefits to others as well as on the benefits to you. What does the headteacher get out of letting you take over the 'monitoring of teaching role' which he or she currently holds? What benefits does the assessment coordinator get out of letting you do the analysis of pupils' attainment and progress instead of holding on to the job? For each of the tasks you have highlighted as being done by others, list the benefits they would receive by passing them to you as subject leader. Consider also the possible disadvantages.

For example, if you would like to take over the analysis of assessment data from the assessment coordinator, the benefits to him or her might include releasing time for other activities. The potential disadvantage is that you might make a mess of things. So how do you ensure that the disadvantages are minimised and the benefits maximised? In the case of assessment, you might need to agree that the assessment coordinator retains overall responsibility but coaches subject leaders in how to do such analyses for their subjects. Together, you devise and implement agreed systems and you report regularly and frequently to the assessment coordinator so that he or she retains a firm whole-school overview. You set targets for improvement within your subject and agree them with the assessment coordinator.

Similarly with monitoring the quality of teaching. What are the benefits to the person currently doing it of giving the role to you? These would include the release of time, again with the potential disadvantage that you might make a poor job of it, upset other teachers and cause a dramatic loss of morale in the school. In this case, you might suggest that you start with some joint monitoring so that you gain from the other person's experience and expertise. Then you agree the systems and formats to be used and report frequently and regularly to your mentor so that he or she is always aware of the situation. You might also identify appropriate in-service training courses for you to attend to improve your technical skills in this area.

The skills needed

The final exercise in this chapter is one which you might like to do as a group with other subject leaders. It requires you to decide which of the skills of subject leadership you need in order to accomplish each of the tasks in the key areas. By completing this task, you will be reinforcing your knowledge and understanding of the national standards before we move on to look at strategies for implementing them in the next chapter. Remember, some of the tasks will require more than a single skill so multiple ticks on any row of the grid on p. 43 are allowed.

Matching skills to tasks

Key area (see pp. 35–37)	Leadership	Decision-making	Communication	Self-management
A1				
A2				
A3				
A4				
A5				
A6				
A7				
B1				
B2				
B3				
B4				
B5				
B6				
B7				
B8				
B9				
B10				
B11				
B12				
B13				
C1				
C2				
C3				
C4				
C5				
C6				
C7				
C8				
C9				
C10				
D1				
D2				
D3				
D4				
D5				
D6				

You should now be in a strong position to identify your priorities in your own professional development. You should be clear where your strengths and weaknesses lie and have some idea of how you can gain the knowledge, understanding and skills you need. Discuss with your staff development coordinator the best way of meeting your training needs through a combination of reading, course attendance and in-school coaching by more experienced staff. Together, draw up a structured programme to ensure that you have the skills needed for effective subject leadership.

So far, you have had a thorough introduction to the national standards for subject leaders. You have had opportunities to evaluate your current impact, role and responsibilities as a subject leader. The rest of this book will give practical guidance on how to carry out your job effectively through:
– establishing the current position of your subject
– identifying priorities for improving it
– devising, implementing and monitoring a subject development plan.

Chapter

5 *Subject audit*

Identifying the starting point

In order to be able to plan the way forward in your subject, you need to know where you are starting from. This will indicate where your priorities lie and help you to devise a manageable and realistic subject development plan. You need to carry out a comprehensive subject audit which will show clearly where the subject is in terms of:
- standards achieved
- progress made by pupils
- quality of provision.

Standards and progress

Each of these aspects can be subdivided to give a more precise indication of the needs of your subject. For example, within standards and progress, you can identify how good they are:
- within lessons
- within key stages
- within year groups
- within gender groups
- within different ability groups
- within the various elements of your subject.

If there are variations, can you identify the causes? Can you identify trends in attainment and progress over recent years? Are standards improving, falling or remaining much the same? How do you know? These are the kinds of questions you will need to ask in order to establish where your subject is and to begin to identify your targets for future developments. Guidance on how to do this is given later. The standards achieved within your subjects are only part of the audit or needs analysis, however. You also need to check why standards are as they are. For example, if you find that standards are either beyond or below those to be expected nationally, can you identify why? The reasons for the standards and for the progress in your subject are largely dependent on the quality of what the school is providing in terms of teaching, the curriculum and assessment procedures and resources for learning. So having got a really good idea of the standards being achieved by pupils in your subject, you next need to analyse why.

Curriculum provision

With curriculum provision, can you identify how good it is in terms of:
- teaching
- curriculum planning
- assessment procedures
- resources
- accommodation?

How does provision appear to be impacting on standards and progress? How do you know? Are there variations in year groups/key stages?

Clearly, such a comprehensive subject audit is a huge task and it requires you to know:
- how you can get the information you need
- how you can present it clearly to those who need it
- how you can use it to improve standards.

When to carry out the audit

Such an audit also requires the cooperation of your colleagues and needs to fit into the whole-school development plan. The school could hardly expect to undertake such a comprehensive analysis of every subject at the same time, so you need to negotiate when your subject is to become a curriculum focus within the whole-school development plan. By phasing the emphasis on subjects, the school will always have some which are being analysed in some depth, others where targets are being set for development and others which are being monitored to check progress towards those targets.

How to get the information

Standards

Having identified what information you require on your subject, you need to consider how you can get it. Starting with standards, try listing some of the ways you could get the evidence you need on the standards being attained by pupils in your subject. Remember that you need to know about standards:
- by the end of each key stage
- within each year group
- of boys and girls
- of different ethnic groups
- of low, average and higher attainers.

Sources of evidence for assessing standards attained in the subject

You might have included some of the following ways of acquiring the information:

- SATS/GCSE results.
- End of year or unit assessment.
- Results of standardised tests.
- Scrutiny of pupils' work.
- Discussions with pupils to check understanding.
- Scrutiny of records of achievement.
- Scrutiny of teachers' mark books and pupil records.
- Scrutiny of portfolios of pupils' levelled work.
- Lesson observations.
- Information from PICSI and PANDA reports.
- Information from your latest inspection report.

Skills needed

Getting and making sense of this information requires certain skills of you as subject leader. Some of these skills are clearly identified in the TTA's standards for subject leaders. For example, you need the ability to analyse data and draw conclusions from it when considering information from published sources like the results of SATs or standardised tests. To get information from some of the other sources requires you to have the ability to secure the cooperation and commitment of your colleagues, some of whom will be more confident than others in letting you have access to it. Consequently, you will require, alongside your analytical skills, well-honed interpersonal skills to enable you to seek some of this information without making less confident colleagues feel insecure.

Devising charts

You need to be well organised to conduct such a comprehensive subject audit, and devising tables and charts on which to collect the information you need can help. For example, to gather the information on standards, you might use a chart like the one illustrated on p. 48.

Audit of standards attained

Subject			
Year group	**NC levels attained** (including variation by gender, ethnicity, ability and between tests and teacher assessments)	**Source of evidence** (test results, pupils' work, records, etc.)	**Evidence** (what do pupils know, understand and do?)
Year			
Year			
Year			
Year			
Year			
Year			
Year			

This will enable you to show, at a glance, the standards being attained by each year group and at the end of each key stage. It will also clearly show how you have come to your judgements on standards. From this information, you can compare your pupils' attainment levels with the expectations of the National Curriculum. You can also see if there are any discrepancies in particular year groups and investigate why this might be. Is it that particular cohort of pupils or is it connected to quality of provision?

Progress

This information also tells you about the progress made by pupils in their learning in each year group. By tabling the levels of attainment by year group in this way, you can see easily where progress is average, or better or worse than average. You can also check the progress of individual pupils by tracking their results in SATs or any standardised tests that the school administers in the subject. You need to ask whether pupils are making the amount of progress they should be making between tests. Do they make a year's progress between annual reading, spelling or number tests, for example? Are any patterns emerging? Does progress seem to be faster or slower than could be expected in particular years or classes or for particular groups of pupils? Do any test results confirm or contradict what pupils are achieving in their class work? Are there any anomalies between teacher assessments and test scores in your subject?

Having tracked attainment and progress – the outcomes – in your subject you need also to check why they are as they are by evaluating the provision.

Auditing curriculum provision

The provision includes all that impacts upon attainment and progress including teaching, curriculum planning, assessment procedures, resources and accommodation.

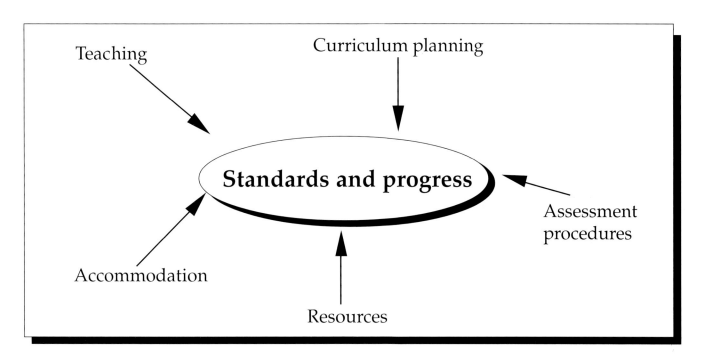

An obvious focus for this aspect of the audit would be to look at any problems highlighted by your standards survey. For example, are there any areas where standards are disappointing or where progress is slower than it should be? If so, you need to know why. Is it just that a particular cohort of pupils do not learn as fast as the others or could it be to do with provision in that year group? A systematic audit of the provision should tell you. Ideally, this will involve separate audits of the various elements of provision and we need to look at each in turn. The most sensible element to begin with is the curriculum, its planning and associated documentation.

Auditing the curriculum

Write down what you think you need to know from an audit of the curriculum. What questions might you want to ask? You might find the OFSTED framework gives you some useful clues here. It requires inspectors to comment in each subject upon:
–   the breadth, balance and relevance of the curriculum
–   whether it provides equality of access to all pupils
–   whether pupils with special educational needs are adequately provided for
–   whether it promotes continuity and progression
–   whether there are adequate and accurate assessment arrangements
–   whether assessment results are used to inform future planning.

How does your subject documentation stand up to scrutiny? What questions would you want to ask about it?

Information needed from a curriculum audit

Your list might have included the following:
- Does the curriculum cover the requirements of the National Curriculum if it is a core subject or information technology (or the requirements of the agreed syllabus for religious education)?
- If it is a foundation subject, is it broad and balanced?
- Is it planned so that pupils build upon what they have learned earlier?
- Do they have the opportunity to revisit themes at more complex levels as they progress through the school?
- Are appropriate learning objectives and activities being set for pupils of these ages?
- Does it support all pupils including those with special educational needs?
- Is there any repetition of work at the same level in different year groups?
- Do policies, schemes of work and planning systems help teachers to know what to teach, how to teach it and when to teach it?
- Does the planning for the subject state clearly what pupils will learn from the activities they will undertake?
- Does the planning include clear and workable strategies for assessing attainment and progress?
- Are assessments used to plan future work?
- Does the curriculum enable all pupils to make good progress?
- Do any pupils miss aspects of the subject for any reasons?
- How useful are the records on pupil attainment and progress?

Information from colleagues

Doing this exercise will give you a clear indication of how effectively the subject is supported by the documentation from your perspective, but it would also be useful to check the perceptions of your colleagues who may not share your level of understanding or enthusiasm for the subject. They can be asked in a staff meeting or by way of a written questionnaire, but you need to be sensitive to the other demands on their time and ensure that they understand:
- what you want to know from them
- when you want to know it
- why you want to know it
- how spending time giving you the information will help them.

However you decide to seek this information from your colleagues, do ensure that it comes to you in a format that is easy to access and is common to all those contributing. If you are seeking written information from your colleagues, devise a simple sheet which will not take them hours to complete and include very clear guidance on what you expect them to do. They will all have more to do than fill in surveys for you! Keep it short and simple.

Summary chart

The information on the curriculum and assessment procedures can be summarised on a grid like the one on p. 52.

Curriculum and assessment audit

	Yes	No	Evidence
Is it broad and balanced, covering the National Curriculum programmes of study where necessary?			
Does it meet statutory requirements?			
Does it promote pupils': – intellectual – physical – personal development?			
Does it provide equality of opportunity for pupils of differing: – ages – ability – gender – ethnicity – social background?			
Does it meet the needs of all pupils with SEN?			
Is long and medium term planning effective in ensuring that all pupils build upon prior learning?			
Is there an effective balance between knowledge, understanding and skills?			
Are there effective systems for: – assessing attainment – recording attainment – analysing assessment data – using assessment information to inform future planning?			

Teaching audit

The other way to check how the subject documentation is helping teachers is to do an audit of the teaching quality which will include:
– a scrutiny of teacher planning
– a scrutiny of pupils' work to check on the value of teachers' marking
– observing teachers in their classrooms.

This is possibly the most sensitive audit you will have to do! Most teachers will now have been observed in their classrooms and had their planning and marking well scrutinised through an external inspection, but this does not mean that they will welcome an internal audit of this kind by the subject leader any more than they welcomed the inspection team. Also, while most inspectors delight in feeding back the positive messages to teachers during the inspection, some are less happy about feeding back the criticisms and difficult messages. It is vital, therefore, that you deal sensitively with this whole area and that any conclusions you make are supported by clear evidence.

Teacher planning

We can break the teaching audit down into three parts, starting with teachers' weekly and daily planning. You will already have evaluated their longer term planning in the audit of the curriculum and, in looking at daily and weekly planning, you need to be aware of how it links in with the longer term plans. In some schools, there is little difference, with the short term planning being little more than a slightly extended list of content from the termly and half-termly plan. In some others, there is excessive planning with repetition between long, medium and short term plans plus policies and schemes of work, all of which contain much the same information. With teachers' short term (weekly and daily) planning, you are looking to see if it says clearly:
– what pupils will learn
– how they will learn it
– how the teacher will know they have learned it.

For this audit, you need each teacher of the subject to let you have copies of his or her short term (weekly and daily) planning for the previous term.

Again, a grid might help you to summarise your findings and pinpoint areas of excellence or weakness. There is an example on the next page for you to consider.

Teachers' daily/weekly planning

Does teachers' planning say clearly ...	... what pupils will learn (clarity of learning objectives)?	... how they will learn it (appropriateness of methodology, differentiation, use of resources)?	... how teachers will know they have learned it (appropriateness of assessment procedures)?
Year			
Year			
Year			
Year			
Year			
Year			
Year			

Common criticisms of teachers' planning from inspections include a lack of clarity in defining precisely what pupils will learn from a particular lesson. Often the learning objectives are so broad as to encompass almost a term's work rather than a single lesson, with some teachers simply copying great chunks from the National Curriculum programmes of study and putting this down as their learning objective. In other cases, teachers' planning says what will be taught rather than what pupils will learn. In some schools, there is a great inconsistency between teachers in the quality of their short term planning. This kind of planning audit can help you as subject leader to identify where poor planning might be affecting classroom performance and where excellent planning might be enhancing it.

Scrutiny of pupils' work

We have already mentioned the benefits of a regular scrutiny of pupils' work in order to assess standards of attainment and the progress pupils make. This scrutiny can also tell you something about the quality of teaching. Given that you are looking at pupils' work purely to give you information about the quality of teaching, what kinds of things might you want to focus on and why? In order to do this audit, you can either take a sample of books from each year group representing the ability range within that year group or, for a really comprehensive audit, you could work through all the books for each group over a longer period. A middle way is to start with a sample from each year group and then to look at more books if you think there are issues with a particular year.

What to look for in pupils' work to help to assess the quality of teaching

What I would look for	Why I would look for it
e.g. Quality of presentation of work	To see if expectations of presentation are high enough
e.g. Quality of marking	To see if it is consistent across classes

From pupils' work, you can look at the quality of the marking and how helpful it is. You can see whether the teacher is enabling all pupils to succeed at their own level or whether they all do the same work in the same way at the same time, which is a fairly common inspection criticism. In this scrutiny, the focus is entirely upon the teaching aspects of the work rather than upon levels of attainment. These factors can again be listed on a grid to make it easy to see any patterns between classes or year groups. There is an example on p. 56.

Scrutiny of pupils' work to look at teaching quality

Year group	Quality of marking (Does it say what is good about the work and how to make it better?)	Continuity (Does the work build effectively upon what has gone before it?)	Level of work and quality of presentation (Does the teacher have high enough expectations of the pupils?)	Differentiation (Is there any evidence of work being effectively differentiated for different abilities?)	Homework (Is it given consistently and does it build effectively upon class work? Is it marked?)
Year					
Year					
Year					
Year					
Year					
Year					
Year					

Teacher observation   Completing these two audits, of planning and pupils' work, should give you some insight into the quality of teaching in the various year groups even before you observe teachers in their classrooms. It might well indicate which classes you ought to focus on if you can only see a limited number in action. For example, you might want to see mainly those where the work and planning scrutinies indicate some issues which are detracting from the high standards you are aiming to achieve. If no issues are obvious from the scrutinies, you may decide to sample classes to give you a spread over the year groups. Observing teachers at work requires you to be able to assess the quality of their work dispassionately against agreed criteria. Some may teach in a similar way to you and consequently there will be the obvious temptation to assume that these are 'good' teachers, while those who teach in a different way are less good. Before beginning, therefore, you need to be very clear about what you are looking for and to ensure that those you are observing are also aware. Try listing the criteria against which you could judge the quality of teaching. What would you be looking for?

Evidence to look for to assess the quality of teaching in a lesson observation

You might have resorted to the OFSTED framework to help you to identify the features of teaching to look for in observing colleagues. The framework identifies eight elements against which teaching should be assessed and also gives useful supporting guidance for each one. The elements are:
– secure subject knowledge
– high expectations
– effective planning
– appropriate methods and organisation
– pupil management and discipline
– effective use of time and resources
– assessment of pupils' work and its use to inform teaching
– use of homework.

Again, putting these elements into a grid format enables you to trace any patterns easily. There is an example below.

Results of teacher observation

Class	
Does the teacher ...	**Evidence**
have secure subject knowledge, including a clear understanding of any National Curriculum requirements?	
set high expectations which challenge all pupils by giving them all hard enough work?	
plan lessons effectively, saying clearly what pupils will learn, how they will learn it and how the teacher will know they have learned it?	
employ methods and strategies which match the objectives of the lessons and the needs of all the pupils?	
manage pupils well, keeping good levels of discipline and behaviour throughout the lesson?	
make effective use of time, through maintaining a good pace to the lesson, and resources, including any support staff?	
assess pupils' work thoroughly and use assessment to inform teaching?	
use homework effectively to reinforce classroom learning?	

Providing feedback

In observing teaching, it is essential that those observing and being observed understand what criteria are being used and it is also helpful to give constructive feedback on teachers through professional dialogue after the lesson. This will include sharing with the individual teachers your perceptions of strengths and weaknesses and some constructive ideas on how they could improve their teaching of your subject.

Resources

The next aspect of your subject audit is resources. You have looked thoroughly at curriculum planning and assessed its impact on standards. You have evaluated the assessment procedures and their application in your subject. You have looked at teachers' planning, marking of work and classroom teaching to see how effective it is. Now you need to see if the resources for your subject are helping or hindering high attainment. Start by listing what you think you need to know from an audit of resources.

Information needed from the resource audit

Subject leaders are usually fairly confident about undertaking a resources audit on the basis that it involves counting things and making lists. However, even the resource audit is not quite as straightforward as just knowing what you have. You also have to make judgements about:

– whether what you have is appropriate
– whether there is enough of it
– whether it is easily accessible
– whether it is of good enough quality
– whether it is effectively used.

So a sheet for helping to audit resources in your subject might look like this:

Resource audit

Subject	What we have (books, tools, materials, artefacts)	Sufficiency (are there enough of each?)	Appropriateness (are they appropriate to the year group?)	Accessibility (are they stored for easy use?)	Quality (what is the quality like?)	Use (are they used effectively in lessons?)
Year						
Year						
Year						
Year						
Year						
Year						
Year						

A sheet like this could be completed by each teacher to check their perception as well as by the subject leader. However, you will need to negotiate with colleagues about checking what they have in their classrooms and stock cupboards. Once you have a list of this type, you can cross-reference it to the standards and progress grids that you have already completed to see if there is any correlation between the adequacy of resources and the standards and progress in particular year groups. You can also relate it to aspects of teaching concerned with the use of resources to see if teachers are in fact using effectively the resources available.

Accommodation

The final audit to undertake is of the accommodation in which your subject is taught. Some subjects clearly require specialist facilities while others can be taught quite effectively within ordinary classrooms. You need to check whether the quality of the accommodation provided for your subject is detracting or enhancing the standards that the pupils achieve. For example, if you are in charge of physical education and find yourself in a school with a purpose-built and fully equipped sports hall, squash courts, tennis courts, hockey court, swimming pool and acres of playing fields, you could reasonably expect to attain higher standards than the school in a cramped inner-city site with poorly modified facilities and not a blade of grass for miles. The crucial issue in assessing the impact of the accommodation on your subject is to check whether it is having an adverse impact on standards. Do not assume that, because you have not got purpose-built everything, the accommodation is inadequate.

Accommodation audit

The questions	Evidence
Is the quality of the accommodation having a positive or negative impact on the standards attained by the pupils?	
Which year groups are affected?	
Are we making effective use of the accommodation that we have?	

Having audited all the various aspects of your subject, you should be quite clear about its current state. You should be very aware of the standards being attained by each year group and the factors influencing those standards. Having gathered the information, you now need to reflect upon it and begin to consider what it all means for the future development of your subject. This will give rise to your position statement and subject development plan which will be the focus of the next chapter.

Chapter

6

The position statement and subject development plan

Producing a position statement

Having undertaken the series of comprehensive audits, you should have a very clear idea of the position of your subject. The next job is to summarise the information. This summary is your subject position statement.

Given that one of the skills of subject leadership is effective self-management, you will have carefully and systematically filed away all the evidence of the audits for easy access. There should be a clear correlation between the outcomes, i.e. standards and progress, and the provision, i.e. teaching, curriculum planning, assessment procedures, resources and accommodation. For example, if you claim that progress in your subject is good in a particular year group, it should follow that teaching is good, as you are unlikely to get good teaching resulting in poor progress. Similarly, poor progress is likely to be the result of poor teaching. If your audit finds a severe shortage of resources but progress and attainment are satisfactory, you need to question whether the resource shortage is as severe as you thought and why it is not impacting more strongly upon standards.

Your position statement needs to reflect these patterns. It needs to be consistent and to be based clearly on the results of the audits.

Report or tables

You can summarise your findings in your position statement either in a simple prose report under the various audit headings or you can produce a series of tables to contain the information, like the examples given below. With these, you need to decide on the descriptors. Are you going to use the inspection scale of well above average to well below average and excellent through to very poor? It would be very helpful if there were a whole-school agreement so that the senior managers could assess priorities between subjects knowing that there was a common language in use.

Table 1: Standards and progress

Standards	Year group	Progress
	Year	
	Year	
	Year	
	Year	
	Year	
	Year	
	Year	
	Pupils with SEN	
	High attainers	
	Girls	
	Boys	
	Ethnic minorities	
	Pupils with English as an additional language	

You might want another table like this indicating the standards by attainment target or for each strand of your subject to show any differences between the various aspects within your subject. The amount of detail and numbers of tables will depend upon the intended audience. The department might need a table for each aspect while the senior management team might only require the overall summary at this stage.

Table 2a: Quality of teaching

Year group	Quality of teaching
Year	
Year	
Year	
Year	
Year	
Year	
Year	

This table gives the overall summary of the teaching quality but you might want to consider another more detailed summary of each aspect of teaching as outlined in the audit that you have done. This would enable you to pick out any patterns across all the teachers and any individual strengths and weaknesses which will determine your staff development plan. An example of the kind of table you might use is given on p.64. You can either use yes/no in the boxes or choose some qualitative descriptors or grades, such as the inspection ones or the ones you used in the self-assessment exercises you did earlier.

Table 2b: Quality of teaching

Does the teacher ...	Teacher A	Teacher B	Teacher C	Teacher D	Teacher E	Teacher F
have secure subject knowledge, including a clear understanding of any National Curriculum requirements?						
set high expectations which challenge all pupils by giving them all hard enough work?						
plan lessons effectively, saying clearly what pupils will learn, how they will learn it and how the teacher will know they have learned it?						
employ methods and strategies which match the objectives of the lessons and the needs of all the pupils?						
manage pupils well, keeping good levels of discipline and behaviour throughout the lesson?						
make effective use of time, through maintaining a good pace to the lesson, and resources, including any support staff?						
assess pupils' work thoroughly and use assessment to inform teaching?						
use homework effectively to reinforce classroom learning?						

Table 3: Curriculum planning and assessment procedures

Curriculum planning		Year group	Assessment procedures		
Long term	Medium term		Accuracy	Use of	Recording
		Year			
		Year			
		Year			
		Year			
		Year			
		Year			
		Year			

This table summarises the quality of planning and assessment in your subject. It highlights any inconsistencies between year groups and between aspects of planning and assessment procedures.

Table 4: Resources and accommodation

Resources			Year group	Accommodation	
Quantity	Quality	Use of		Quality	Use of
			Year		
			Year		
			Year		
			Year		
			Year		
			Year		
			Year		

This table tells you whether you have sufficient good quality resources and accommodation in your subject. It will also highlight how effectively year groups use them.

Strengths and weaknesses

These tables now provide your basic subject position statement. You can develop this by summarising, from these tables, the strengths and weaknesses in your subject. An example is given below. Your subject position statement can be presented just as the series of tables or you can turn it into a more sophisticated report for specific audiences. The important thing to remember is that it should summarise the current state of your subject under each of the headings used throughout the audits. It should be a helpful working tool not an attempt to dazzle the senior management team with your desktop publishing skills!

Example of strengths and weaknesses in the subject

	Strengths	**Weaknesses**
Standards	Achievement of girls at GCSE Numbers achieving a GCSE pass	Achievement of boys at GCSE Numbers achieving higher grades at GCSE
Progress	Progress of pupils with SEN Progress of girls in GCSE groups	Progress of more able pupils Progress of the lower attainers who do not have SEN
Teaching	Subject knowledge Control and discipline of pupils Use of resources	Use of marking to inform planning Differentiation within lessons
Curriculum planning	Long term planning which ensures progression through syllabus	Planning for differentiation
Assessment procedures	End of unit tests	Ongoing teacher assessment Use of assessment to inform future planning
Resources	New text books in Years _____	Lack of practical equipment for Years _____
Accommodation	Size of the classrooms means plenty of space for independent research	Leaky mobiles mean that in wet weather we can only use half of each classroom

Having identified the strengths and weaknesses, you need to make sure that all those who teach the subject also recognise them. You will have been feeding back during the audits so that staff should not be surprised by the final position statement or the strengths and weaknesses list. However, you should make sure that everyone concerned with teaching the subject recognises what needs to be done and why it needs to be done. This is where you rely upon your well-honed communication skills! You need to share this information, not in order to apportion blame but to make sure that all of the team supports the development plan. Meeting all the targets identified within the plan will be a team effort and the more involvement the team has in devising it, the greater will be everyone's sense of ownership. While you will do the bulk of the work on it, the plan needs to be accepted as the *team's* development plan rather than yours which the team reluctantly goes along with.

Sharing the subject position statement

You need to decide who to share your position statement with, as this will dictate its format. Remember to match the message to the audience and choose the most appropriate medium. In the following exercise, list who needs to know the position of your subject, why they need to know it and how you might best present it to them.

Who needs to know?	Why do they need to know?	How is it best presented?
The subject leader	You have responsibility for improving standards in your subject	

Clearly, you need to know and, although you should have the bulk of the information at your fingertips, you need to know in a format which enables you to see easily where the strengths and weaknesses lie. This might require a simple series of tables like those suggested. Those who teach the subject need to know because it is through them that you will improve standards unless you are a one-person subject department. Your colleagues will want to see at a glance the significance of all the audits that they have been involved in but they might also appreciate a bit of the evidence too. In this case, you might share with them the results of the audits through a staff meeting so that they can discuss with you how you have arrived at the position statement. This is also useful for ensuring that they agree with the position statement in order that they see the relevance of the subject development plan arising from it.

The head, senior managers and governors might need to see your position statement in order to be aware of possible resource implications arising from your forthcoming development plan and to set your subject priorities from their perspective into the whole-school priorities. The format here needs to be as accessible as possible and there may be an agreed school format. These people will no more appreciate a very heavy, very lengthy report than anyone else will, so avoid the temptation to try to impress with quantity rather than quality!

Other subject leaders and teachers with specific responsibilities might need to know the position of your subject in relation to their role. For example, the special needs coordinator might require information on any issues you have discovered relating to pupils with special educational needs. The teacher in charge of information and communications technology might need to know about issues relating to the use of ICT in your subject. The teachers in charge of English and mathematics might appreciate knowing about issues affecting literacy and numeracy skills in your subject so that they can take them into account when drawing up their own subject development plans. Those with responsibility for the whole-school curriculum, for assessment and for staff development might need to know the position of your subject in relation to their areas. Each of these people will require specific information on your subject in relation to their own particular responsibilities and may not appreciate a full version of the statement.

Parents might need to know the position of your subject in so far as it directly affects them through issues like homework, for example. They might also be very interested in a clear statement on standards and progress but might be less interested in some of the more detailed aspects of the provision. Your subject adviser might appreciate a summary of your position statement so that she or he can offer constructive advice on devising your subject development plan.

You might well have identified other groups and individuals with a need to know. The important thing is to communicate your position statement in a form which makes it easily accessible to them. Work out why they need the information and then how best they might like it. Ask them, if necessary, rather than going to a great deal of effort to produce a delightful report in a format that you find pleasing but that is irrelevant to the recipients. Remember that this is not just an opportunity to blow your own trumpet but is also the basis of your subject development plan which will outline how you intend to improve standards in your subject over the next few years.

The subject development plan

Deciding what to include

You can discuss the audits and the position statement in a series of staff meetings with those who teach the subject. This is a good opportunity to practise what you have learned about running effective meetings and leading staff. See if you can draw up a programme of meetings for:
- disseminating the information you have gathered from the audits you have carried out
- agreeing the position statement
- agreeing the main weaknesses of the subject
- agreeing the issues which have to be addressed
- agreeing the issues that you would like to address
- agreeing how you might address these issues.

An example of the agenda for the first meeting is given on p. 69.

Agenda for first meeting

Meeting Subject development planning meeting	Date Time Venue Purpose To agree the subject position statement and identify the main issues we need to address in the subject development plan.	Those attending All those involved in the teaching and support of the subject.

Agenda item	Item leader	Time needed	Discussion, decision or information
1. The draft position statement	Subject leader	30 mins	Decision
2. Initial identification of the main issues	Subject leader	60 mins	Discussion
3.			
4.			
5.			
Pre-meeting preparation, papers attached. Copy of the draft subject position statement.			

It would be useful to have a flipchart handy to record the ideas generated, with the results being typed and circulated before the following meeting. As a result of these meetings, you should be able to draw up an agreed list of what you *have to* put in your development plan and what you, the department, *would like to* put in. For example, you *might like to* target improved resources in order to further improve standards which are currently satisfactory. However, you might *have to* target curriculum planning which is causing progress in some year groups to be less than satisfactory. The *have to* issues arise from the weaknesses that you have identified within your position statement and the *want to* issues arise from the relative strengths.

Exercise on identifying targets

The next exercise gives you the opportunity to identify targets for improvement in a hypothetical case study.

Try using the weaknesses from the strengths and weaknesses example given on p. 66 to draw up a list of targets that you would have to address if they related to your subject. Some ideas have been included already on the following chart.

	Weaknesses	Targets for improvement
Standards	1. Achievement of boys at GCSE 2. Numbers achieving higher grades at GCSE	2. Increase the numbers achieving higher GCSE grades by ...
Progress	1. Progress of more able pupils 2. Progress of the lower attainers who do not have SEN	
Teaching	1. Use of marking to inform planning 2. Differentiation within lessons	1. Improve the use of marking through: – revising the marking policy to include clearer guidance on using marking to inform planning – a staff training session to introduce revised policy and how to make best use of it
Curriculum planning	1. Planning for differentiation	1. Improve planning for differentiation through: – clearer guidance in subject policy and schemes of work – staff training on planning for differentiation
Assessment procedures	1. Ongoing teacher assessment 2. Use of assessment to inform future planning	
Resources	1. Lack of practical equipment for Years _____	
Accommodation	1. Leaky mobiles mean that in wet weather we can only use half of each classroom	

Possible other targets Having focused on the weaknesses, there may be some areas of the provision which are currently satisfactory but which you would like to improve in order to raise standards even further. For example, you might like more resources for a particular aspect of your subject. In drawing up these targets, you need to be very clear on the impact they will have. If you have extra resources, books or materials, how do you expect them to impact on the standards the pupils are achieving? It may be that with more books you could provide greater opportunities for independent research for the more able pupils. This would allow teachers to work more closely with the less able, thus potentially improving the standards achieved by both groups. Or perhaps you only have enough resources because the staff spend a lot of time producing them. Buying resources in would release staff time for other aspects of their work and be more cost-effective (remember the cost of staff time).

The format of the subject development plan

Having established the state of your subject through the audits and the subject position statement, you are now well placed to devise your subject development plan. This is the tool that you will use to drive standards up by improving the quality of provision. There may be an accepted school format for subject development planning which indicates the information you need to include. If there is not, try listing the kind of information that you think you will need to include.

Information to include in the subject development plan

_____

_____

_____

_____

_____

_____

_____

_____

_____

_____

_____

Your development plan must include:
– clear targets which say what you will achieve
– agreed deadlines by which you will meet your targets
– how you will meet them
– the cost of meeting them
– how you will know that you have met them.

It may also need to include the name of the person responsible for implementing particular aspects of the plan if parts of it are to be delegated. Avoid making it too complicated though. This is a working tool, not a work of art.

You might find the example given on the next page a useful suggestion.

Example of a simple grid to summarise your plan

Target	Deadline	Method	Cost	Success criteria
1.				
2.				
3.				
4.				
5.				
6.				
7. etc.				

Targets

In a nutshell, targets need to be:
- measurable
- achievable
- specific
- time-related.

Development planning is rather like a journey. You know where you are starting from (and if you don't, you find out!). You know, or decide, where you need to go. Having decided your destination, you plan how you might get there and how long it will take. The destination is your target and the way you decide to get there is your method. As in planning any journey, you need to express your targets in very specific terms.

A target of 'raising standards within the subject' is equivalent to a journey 'up North'. How are you going to know when you get there? Where is 'up North'? Your journey is more likely to be to a specific location, an office, a school or a hotel in Aberdeen, Edinburgh or Newcastle rather than just 'up North'. Instead of just 'raising standards', you need to define by how much you are going to raise standards and when you will have achieved this. For example, a clearer target for improved standards might be:
- to raise the percentage of pupils achieving grades A to C at GCSE from 55% to 70% within four years, or
- to raise the percentage of pupils attaining level _____ in the end of key stage assessments from 45% to 60% within four years.

Each time you set a target in your development plan, ask yourself whether it is clear enough. Will you know when you have reached it?

Deadline

Staying with the comparison between development planning and a journey, you rarely set off somewhere without some fairly clear idea of when you will arrive. There are times when things crop up to delay you and you need to alter your arrangements but you normally have a timescale for the journey when you are planning it.

So it is with your subject development plan. Set dates by which you will have achieved your targets. Again be specific. Deadlines focus the mind and ensure that you stay on course. Think of all those jobs you are going to do 'sometime' which never get done and compare them to the ones with a deadline attached, like decorating the lounge before the friends come to stay or having a policy in place before the inspection team arrives! You need to make your deadlines realistic but challenging. You might like to have policies in place before an inspection but if it starts tomorrow, you might find your deadline too challenging! Equally, if your inspection is four years away, you might find that deadline too far in the other direction.

Method

This is the meat of your plan. This is where you spell out the steps that you will take to achieve your targets within your set timescale. In the case of a journey, this is where you get out the maps and plans and decide your route, whether to drive or take the train, use the motorway or the back roads. In this section, you will list the actions that you will set in motion in order to achieve each of your targets. This might include staff development through in-service training, revising policy documents to offer more guidance to staff, developing or buying more resources to replace those of poor quality and so on. The way you achieve your targets depends on what your targets are and the resources you have available or can secure from the senior management team to fund your subject development plan.

Cost

Everything costs. Even when you think you are saving money by doing a job yourself, you need to bear in mind the cost of your time and that of other people. The following chart gives some indication of the cost of time so that you can see the true cost of a full day departmental meeting, for example. In devising your plan, you need to be sensitive to the need to get value for money. So if you take the entire subject department on a day course which is only really relevant to half of them, you have not only wasted the course fees but also a lot of people's valuable time which has a monetary value. When costing the various parts of your plan, ensure that you include the staffing costs. After all, the staff could be doing something else with that time.

Salary	5 mins	15 mins	1 hour	1 day
£35,000	£1.75	£5.25	£21.00	£147
£30,000	£1.50	£4.50	£18.00	£126
£25,000	£1.25	£3.75	£15.00	£105
£20,000	£1.00	£3.00	£12.00	£84
£15,000	£0.75	£2.25	£9.00	£63
£10,000	£0.50	£1.50	£6.00	£42

Success criteria

You need to have a mechanism within your plan to measure how successful you have been. This includes not only achieving your targets but also the impact of achieving them on standards and the progress of pupils. For example, your development plan might include a target of producing a policy on marking. Once you have the policy written and in place, you have reached your target and achieved that objective. However, unless that policy helps to raise standards, there was little point in writing it. Having written it, can you really breathe a sigh of relief, tick it off your list and let it lie on bookshelves unused for years?

You need to include within your development plan clear success criteria which refer to the impact of each element of the plan on standards. Otherwise, you could achieve all your targets without having the slightest impact on the performance of pupils. You could produce dozens of policy documents which are never referred to and planning systems which are never used. What might be the success criteria for having developed an agreed marking policy? Possibly something along the lines of 'higher standards as pupils have a clearer idea of what is good about their work and what they need to do to make it better'.

A case study

Let us conclude this chapter with an opportunity to work through from what was observed in auditing to setting targets in the development plan in a hypothetical case study.

The following exercise illustrates the way the audits lead to the position statement and on to the development plan. Try working through from what was observed in the audits to targets for improvement in the example on p. 75. Here, the observation concerns mixed ability teaching.

Exercise in development planning

Audit (What I observed)	Position statement (What this means in terms of outcomes, i.e. standards and progress of pupils)	Position statement (What this means in terms of educational provision, i.e. teaching, curriculum planning, assessment procedures, resources and accommodation)	Development plan (Issues for the development plan)
All pupils in a mixed ability class doing exactly the same work at the same level in lessons. Their books showed that this is the normal pattern.		**Teaching**	**Teaching**
		Curriculum planning	**Curriculum planning**
		Assessment procedures	**Assessment procedures**
		Resources	**Resources**
		Accommodation	**Accommodation**

Hypothetical answer

Audit (What I observed)	Position statement (What this means in terms of outcomes, i.e. standards and progress of pupils)	Position statement (What this might mean in terms of educational provision, i.e. teaching, curriculum planning, assessment procedures, resources and accommodation)	Development plan (Possible issues for the development plan)
All pupils in a mixed ability class doing exactly the same work at the same level in lessons. Their books showed that this is the normal pattern.	Work is not well matched to individual abilities so that the higher attainers are not being challenged sufficiently. As a consequence, they are not achieving the standards of which they are capable.	**Teaching** 1. Teachers are not skilled at working with mixed ability groups. 2. They are not providing opportunities for independent working. 3. They are not providing extension activities for more able pupils.	**Teaching** In-service training on: 1. working with mixed ability groups 2. providing opportunities for independent working 3. meeting the needs of more able pupils.
		Curriculum planning 1. Teachers are not planning work for different abilities. 2. There is insufficient guidance in the subject documentation to guide teacher planning.	**Curriculum planning** 1. In-service training on planning for mixed ability groups. 2. Revise subject policy to give clearer guidance on planning for differentiation.
		Assessment procedures Teachers are not using assessment effectively to prepare work which is well matched to pupils' abilities.	**Assessment procedures** Revise assessment procedures and check teacher planning to see that they are using them to plan future work.
		Resources There is not enough material at different levels for some of the areas covered.	**Resources** Create working parties to develop materials for different abilities on common themes. Check catalogues for resources.
		Accommodation	**Accommodation** No issues

When transferring this information to the subject development planning format, the grid might look like this.

Development plan for case study

Target	Deadline	Method	Cost	Success criteria
1. To raise the standards of the higher attainers.	Within a year.	**Teaching** In-service training on: 1. working with mixed ability groups 2. providing opportunities for independent working 3. meeting the needs of more able pupils.		Higher attainers will reach higher standards because they will be given harder work.
		Curriculum planning 1. In-service training on planning for mixed ability groups. 2. Revise subject policy to give clearer guidance on planning for differentiation.		
		Assessment procedures Revise assessment procedures and check teacher planning to see that they are using them to plan future work.		
		Resources Create working parties to develop materials for different abilities on common themes. Check catalogues for resources.		
		Accommodation No issues		

This is an example of addressing identified weaknesses in your subject. By focusing on the issue, you are attempting initially to bring standards up to a satisfactory level. You might identify issues that are currently satisfactory and which you want to improve upon. For example, although the percentage of your pupils achieving levels A to C at GCSE is in line with the national average, your target might be to raise it by 15% over the next four years. In this case, the relevant part of your subject development plan might look like the one on p. 78.

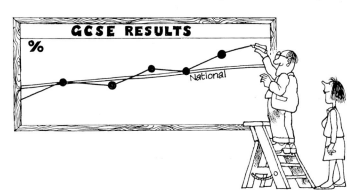

Plan for improving GCSE results

Target	Deadline	Method	Cost	Success criteria
To increase the percentage of pupils gaining A to C passes by 15%.	Within four years.	1. Setting targets for all pupils based upon their end of Key Stage 3 assessments.		
		2. Regularly monitoring progress towards these targets.		
		3. Extra support for those on the border between a D and a C pass.		
		4. etc.		

In this chapter, you have looked at ways of summarising the information from your subject audits so that those who need it can access it easily. You have worked through the requirements of an effective subject development plan with its emphasis on clear targets within an agreed timescale and on success criteria which state what impact the targets will have on the standards that pupils achieve. You have considered who to involve in devising the subject plan and how to involve them and you have tracked an issue from observing pupils at work through to the issues for the subject development plan. In the next chapter, you will look at how you implement the plan and get people to achieve the targets that have been agreed.

Chapter

7

Implementing and monitoring the subject development plan

Having looked at some of the strategies for devising and producing a subject development plan, this chapter will focus on how to implement it and how to monitor its progress. It will encourage you to distinguish between leadership, management and administration and between maintenance tasks and those which take the subject forward. Development requires change and this chapter will include some guidance on managing change effectively. As subject development planning involves a series of projects, it will also incorporate some guidance on effective project management.

Managing the subject development plan

Implementing the subject development plan requires you to use your skills of leadership, management and administration. Many managers mistake administrative tasks for management. Having taken on a position of responsibility, they get sidetracked by the paperwork that comes with it rather than focusing on management tasks. This is a particular temptation in teaching when so much of the class teacher's role is a management one. Moving up to a position of responsibility involves doing different things and the things that are obviously different are often the routine administrative tasks. So try to distinguish the differences between leadership, management and administration. In the space below, try to define the key factors of each.

Differences between leadership, management and administration

Leadership	Management	Administration

Leadership

Leadership has many dictionary definitions but the most appropriate one in this context is to do with causing people to go along with oneself. Clearly, you can do that by roping them together and dragging them whether they want to go with you or not, but effective leadership is about influencing or inspiring people so that they want to accompany you. It involves having a clear vision for the future and a clear sense of direction which is conveyed to followers. The emphasis is on your interpersonal role, your ability to influence and motivate other people. Leadership has a strong focus on:

– style
– staff
– skills
– shared goals.

Management

Management is about controlling the course of affairs and attaining the set objectives. It is about getting things done through other people in order to achieve stated organisational objectives. Management therefore focuses on:

– strategy
– structures
– systems.

There is sometimes a confusion about the difference between managing and doing. Managing is much more about:

– clarifying objectives
– planning the work
– organising the distribution of activities and tasks
– directing staff
– controlling the performance of other people's work.

You can see from this list just how much of the class teacher's job is a management one. It is a profession where you enter at management level with the responsibilities outlined above, whereas in many others you start very much below this level, with much of your work being directed by others. Gaining promotion in teaching usually means taking on a role involving managing other adults as well as your pupils. Many of the skills required are the same except that you are dealing with an older set of people.

Administration

Administration is the carrying out of tasks in line with the wishes or demands of management. It is the operation of procedures used by management to get things done. It can be seen as tasks taking place according to a set of rules and procedures, while management has a much greater degree of discretion.

Implementing your subject development plan requires an appropriate balance between leadership, management and administration. Clearly, there will be routine paperwork involved, ordering and invoicing, completing forms and so on. There will also be much management in terms of organising, directing and controlling tasks, activities and people. And of course you will find it very difficult to improve your subject without the leadership skills to take your people forward with you. The important thing is to get the balance correct and to avoid getting bogged down in the routine tasks which have little influence on development.

Try the following exercise to see how the balance is at the moment, based upon your current job description. List, in the first column, all the tasks from your job description and then tick according to whether they are leadership, management or administrative tasks.

Job description	Leadership	Management	Administration

Maintenance and development tasks

As subject leader, you will find that some of the tasks you undertake have a significant impact on taking the subject forward or developing it while others are more concerned with maintaining things as they are. For example, the subject development plan is, by its very nature, designed to promote planned changes in the subject and the way it is delivered. It is a *development task* which results in changes. Ordering basic stock like pencils and paper on the other hand is a *maintenance task*. Without it, the subject would falter and pupils would not be able to work effectively but it hardly has a dramatic effect on changing the subject or raising standards. The effective subject leader will ensure an appropriate balance between maintenance and development tasks. There will be some natural overlap between the two types and some tasks which begin as development ones will become maintenance ones as the subject moves forward and new innovations become accepted practice.

Maintenance tasks which ensure the smooth running of the subject.

Development tasks which take the subject forward and promote change.

Many of the maintenance tasks will be routine administrative ones, while many of the development tasks will fall under the headings of leadership and management.

In implementing your subject development plan, you are naturally focusing on development activities. Consequently, much of what is involved comes under the leadership and management headings but there will still be routine administration to keep up to date in terms of systems and procedures. Try to ensure that these are as simple as possible and that they do not take an excessive amount of time which could be devoted to leading and managing your subject to even greater heights. An example of how your subject development plan encompasses all three areas is given below.

Example showing the use of all three skills

Plan	Leadership	Management	Administration
To improve the quality of teaching by: – regular observation of and feedback to teachers in the classrooms – in-service training in planning for differentiation – regular analysis of pupils' work and teacher planning to check for evidence of effective differentiation.	As leader, you will have to ensure that the staff involved share your vision for improving the subject, understand the importance of these aspects of the plan and are convinced that they are worth doing. You will have to convince staff that the kind of rigorous scrutiny involved is going to be worthwhile in terms which they can appreciate.	As manager, you will have to plan the programme of observations and scrutinies, taking into account other factors which may have a bearing, e.g. timetables. You will have to devise the systems necessary to accomplish these tasks. You will have to direct staff in terms of what you require and when you require it.	As administrator, you will have to complete the various forms and pieces of paper which constitute a record of the observations and scrutinies and complete records showing your findings.

It may be that these items from your subject development plan are new and have not been a feature of the subject before. At this stage, therefore, they are definitely development tasks designed to take the subject forward. You and your colleagues may decide that the benefits from such observations and scrutinies are so worthwhile that you adopt them as regular ongoing practice. They now move from the purely development category partly into the maintenance one. They become an essential part of the way you ensure that the quality you are offering is maintained.

Project management

Your subject development plan is a series of projects. A project is different to everyday work for a number of reasons:
● It has a specific purpose and objectives.
● It has a clearly determined life cycle with start and end dates fixed.
● It is likely to lead to some change.

A project works to a cycle including four distinct phases: planning, implementation, completion and review. Having produced your subject development plan, you should have completed the first stage of the project which included:
– setting objectives
– identifying ways of achieving them
– outlining tasks to be completed
– setting timescales
– identifying resources required
– agreeing the plan with those it concerns.

Implementing the plan involves actually doing the work set out in the planning stage. This involves:
– agreeing tasks with people
– doing the work
– monitoring and reviewing progress
– modifying plans in the light of experience where necessary
– regular communication with the team.

Completion of your project is when you have achieved the targets that you set at the planning stage. In this respect, you could complete your subject plan and then start planning the next. In reality, what you will do is to review each section of it as it is completed and regularly update the plan in the light of these reviews. In this way, your plan is a dynamic working tool and never actually comes to an end. It rolls forward from year to year as each element is completed and gives rise to another innovation. The model below illustrates the cycle.

The project cycle

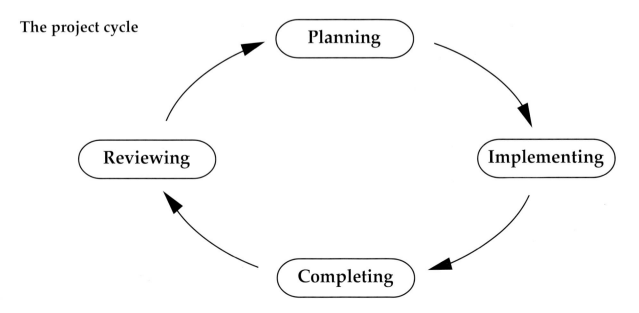

Discrete tasks of a project

Any project is a series of discrete tasks. Within your subject development plan, you will have a whole series of projects under each of the headings that we have been using throughout this book:

- Standards.
- Progress.
- Teaching.
- Curriculum planning.
- Assessment procedures.
- Resources.
- Accommodation.

Each can be broken down into its discrete tasks and, indeed, needs to be to make it more manageable. Some of the tasks can be undertaken concurrently and some need to be completed before others can begin. It is important that you are well organised and have your timescales worked out so that staff are not overburdened by having several innovations to handle at once. There are various ways of showing the route of your subject plan to ensure that the work is well balanced over the year and that each project within it is planned systematically in the most appropriate order. One of the simplest is the Gantt chart, devised by Henry Lawrence Gantt in the First World War. It shows the sequence of tasks, parallel tasks, dependent tasks and the time each needs.

A Gantt chart

Week	1	2	3	4	5	6	7	8	9	10	11	12	13	14
Task A	▨	▨	▨											
Task B			▨	▨										
Task C					▨	▨	▨							
Task D					▨	▨								
Task E								▨						
Task F										▨	▨	▨		
Task G											▨	▨	▨	
Task H												▨	▨	
Task I												▨	▨	▨

This shows that Task A needs to be two-thirds completed before you can begin Task B. Tasks C and D cannot begin until Tasks A and B are complete. Task C can run concurrently with Task D. In order to complete a Gantt chart, you need to break down each of your projects into its list of discrete tasks. You then need to decide how long each task is likely to take, which tasks are dependent on others and which can run concurrently.

Using a Gantt chart

Try the following exercise. Assume you have been given the task of producing the end of term school play and have to organise everything from writing the script through to the actual performances in front of parents and governors. What would your Gantt chart for the project look like?

The chart given includes a range of the tasks and has been partly completed for you. See if you can finish it so that everything is allocated to its correct place in the project thus ensuring that the play goes on according to schedule.

Tasks	Wk 1	Wk 2	Wk 3	Wk 4	Wk 5	Wk 6	Wk 7	Wk 8	Wk 9	Wk 10	Wk 11
Write script	▓	▓									
Have it typed		▓	▓								
Have it copied			▓								
Book hall	▓										
Inform parents		▓									
Audition				▓							
Make costumes											
Make props											
Design set											
Make set											
Rehearse actors											
Recruit backstage											
Rehearse backstage											
Get make-up											
Rehearse make-up											
Print tickets											
etc.											

Having this kind of overview of each aspect of your subject development plan can also help you to avoid clashes between the different elements. For example, if you are working on revising subject guidance, policies and schemes of work under the curriculum heading, you might want to ensure that this work is completed before you start the working parties on producing extra resources for higher attainers or designing end of unit assessments. You can also use a similar chart to check the workload on staff by listing tasks down the left-hand side as normal and listing staff involved in them across the top. By blocking out the boxes where staff are involved in particular tasks, you can see if anyone has an excessive workload compared to the other staff.

Gantt charts also serve as a useful monitoring system. By knowing when each task should have been completed, you can easily see at a glance whether each element of your overall plan is on schedule or not. If you find certain bits are going faster or slower than you anticipated, you can take action to get back on track. This assumes, of course, that having produced your plan and your Gantt charts, you have planned in regular times to review how much progress is being made at specific points!

Agreeing tasks with people

Another element of the successful project is agreeing tasks with people. You should have done some of this at the planning stage. However, there might have been occasions at that stage when you were selling your plan to staff and they agreed with you rather than arguing. When it comes down to actually going on the course or taking part in the staff workshop, you might find that what you thought was straightforward has suddenly become rather more complicated – the staff now assume they don't actually need it. This is where your leadership skills are tested, particularly your communication skills.

If you are having difficulties getting staff to implement various parts of the subject plan, you need to look first of all at the reasons for their reluctance. Even though they seemed to agree with the plan when you presented it to them, they may have said one thing verbally and another non-verbally. You need to be aware of the real messages you and others are giving and receiving in face-to-face communication. There is not scope to go into the detail of body language in this book but you do need to be aware of some basic background.

Body language

A knowledge of body language is important because it accounts for up to 80% of the message in face-to-face communication, while tone of voice and the actual words account for the remaining 20%. Body language never lies so that if someone says one thing verbally and another non-verbally, the non-verbal message is the correct one. Think how often you have tried to pay someone an insincere compliment which has backfired. Although your words were favourable, your gestures gave the game away.

Body language reinforces attitudes. If you have staff who are unsure about aspects of your plan, they may agree at the planning stage because that is easier than arguing. However, they will adopt negative body language in doing so. As long as they adopt negative body language in response to that element, they will continue to feel negative towards it. Change their stance and you change their attitude. For example, if you are holding a meeting at which the staff feel anxious and adopt barriers like crossed arms, as long as they maintain the crossed arms they will continue to feel negative. You need to get them to remove the barriers and they will respond more positively. In this instance, the simplest way is to circulate something which has to be passed on, like a packet of mints or a plate of biscuits. They cannot pass on the mints or biscuits with their arms folded so they open them. By opening them, they change their attitude and if you time it well, you can persuade them to stay more open and responsive.

When talking to colleagues, you can be aware of changes of posture and stance which might indicate a change from a negative to a positive state of mind. Equally, if your listener dislikes something you have said, you may notice a tendency to put up barriers at that particular moment. Improving your knowledge of such gestures and their meanings will help you to understand people better and to communicate more effectively with them. Open palms are accepted as a sign of sincerity so do not try 'selling' your ideas to people while your hands are firmly in your pockets.

Physical position

The physical position you adopt in relation to the other person will also have a bearing on how receptive the listener may be. For example, if you ask a member of staff to get involved in a particular part of your subject development plan, the seating arrangement you use can have an impact on how well your message is received. We normally choose to sit directly facing the other person over a desk when we are in a competitive mood, as in playing chess for instance. When we are working together on the crossword puzzle, this position would not be appropriate so we choose the more co-operative one of sitting alongside the other person or at least around a corner of the table. It is also important to avoid having chairs of different heights which might make the other person feel inferior or put down.

The diagram below illustrates the confrontational or competitive position and the co-operative one.

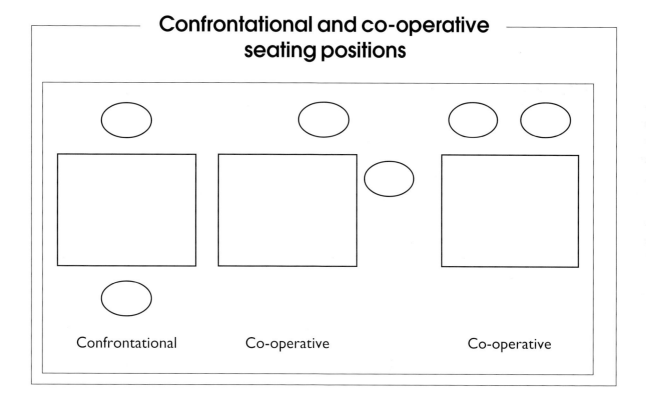

Confrontational and co-operative seating positions

Confrontational   Co-operative   Co-operative

Language choice

As well as being aware of non-verbal communication, you can also make implementation easier by being aware of your own and other people's preferred language choices. Research indicates that everyone uses words associated with the senses and that most people express a particular preference for words which are either visual or auditory or kinaesthetic (to do with touch). If you normally use visual terms, you will get on well with others who also use visual terms but less well with someone who favours auditory language. The most effective communicators are those who always use a variety of visual, auditory and kinaesthetic vocabulary. Try the following exercise in which you have to think of as many terms as possible for each column according to the sense to which they refer. There are some examples to start you off.

Visual	Auditory	Kinaesthetic
See what I mean?	That sounds okay.	That doesn't feel right.
That looks okay.	That rings a bell.	How does that strike you?
Do you get the picture?		

Visual examples

Under the visual heading, you might have come up with terms like these:
- I see that now.
- That looks right.
- Let's get this into perspective.
- I'm still in the dark on this.
- I get the picture.
- Can you picture that?
- What is your view?
- All will be revealed ...
- What kind of image do you want to create?
- My vision for the future ...

Auditory examples

Under the auditory heading, you might have come up with terms like these:
- I get the message.
- Does that sound okay?
- Listen to me.
- I hear what you're saying.
- That strikes a chord.
- It suddenly clicked.
- Something tells me that's not right.
- That's music to my ears.

Kinaesthetic examples

Under the kinaesthetic heading, you might have come up with terms like these:
- How does that strike/grab you?
- Can you relate to that?
- How does that impact on ...
- I can't handle that.
- I am getting a taste for this.
- I smell a rat.
- It makes my skin creep.
- Let me give you a concrete example.
- It is difficult to handle.
- She has a firm grasp of the situation.

Listen to the kinds of words that you use regularly and note which your preferred sense is. Make a point of listening out for these key words in conversations that you have over the next few weeks to see (visual!) if you can work out the preferences of those around you. Try listening when you are out with friends socially and pick up (kinaesthetic!) the range in use among your friends.

People are normally attracted to people like themselves, so if you use visual terms a lot, you are likely to get on better with visual people. This does mean that you might have difficulty in getting the message across to your auditory and kinaesthetic counterparts. In the extreme, such communication problems can lead to separation, where one partner constantly makes visual references like 'I don't see what's wrong ...', while the other always uses auditory ones like 'well, if you'd only listen ...'.

If you think you might have difficulties related to these ideas, you could always draw up a chart like the one on p. 90 and actually record the preferences you hear around the school. Why not try working on the chart together with your colleagues?

Person's name	Visual	Auditory	Kinaesthetic

Motivators

Implementing your subject development plan requires more than just effective communication skills. It also requires you to motivate those involved enough to do what is needed to ensure that your plan is successful. Some may be well motivated by the tasks assigned to them while others are not. This may be because of the terms in which you have expressed the plan.

Herzberg's two factor theory

There are many theories of motivation and it is beyond the scope of this book to delve into them in any depth. One theory which might have a bearing is Herzberg's two factor theory in which he identifies hygiene or maintenance factors and motivators or growth factors. The theory is that people will be dissatisfied if the hygiene factors are lacking but just attending to them does not result in satisfaction, merely in the absence of dissatisfaction. To have a satisfied and motivated workforce, you need to ensure that both the sources of dissatisfaction and the sources of satisfaction or motivation are attended to. Herzberg lists as the dissatisfiers (hygiene or maintenance factors):
– salary
– job security
– working conditions
– level and quality of supervision
– company policy and administration
– interpersonal relations.

These include factors which are often assumed to be keys to effective motivation, the idea being that more money, for example, will improve morale and lead to a more motivated workforce. According to Herzberg, it will simply lead to less dissatisfaction. He identifies the motivators or growth factors, those elements which lead people to enjoy job satisfaction, as:
– personal growth and advancement
– nature of the work
– responsibility
– recognition
– sense of achievement.

There is probably little that you can do personally about the dissatisfiers, as many of these are beyond your remit as subject leader. However, you can focus on the motivators and ensure that those involved in implementing your subject development plan receive a sense of achievement and some recognition. Your task is to ensure that the sense of achievement and recognition are in a form acceptable to each individual. You might have colleagues who would be highly motivated by the prospect of recognition in the form of a prestigious award ceremony. Others would shudder at the prospect. There will be those who are motivated by the very nature of the tasks you have given them and others who require some external motivators to get them fully involved. The effective leader recognises the individuality of each member of staff and knows how to motivate them.

Effective management

In traditional management (and teaching), you give people tasks, follow their progress on them and then criticise them as soon as they make a mistake. In effective management, you give them the tasks and follow their progress until you find them doing something right and then praise them for it. In this way, you are not only recognising achievement, you are also building self-esteem, which is an essential part of any leader's role.

If you do have to tackle someone over something he or she has not done properly, you need to criticise the behaviour, not the person. You need to say what was wrong, why it was wrong and what needs to be done to make it right. You always leave the person that you have reprimanded with a positive message. Having criticised the behaviour, you express a positive view about his or her ability to correct it. Adults will live up or down to your expectations just as pupils will. If you show that you have high expectations, they will respond appropriately. If you are always criticising people, they will lose faith in their ability and believe that they can't cope. You will have come across this with people who say things like 'I'm only a ...' or with pupils who believe that 'kids like me can't do this stuff.' As a leader, you have to ensure that people working with you have appropriate self-esteem. This can be illustrated in the following model.

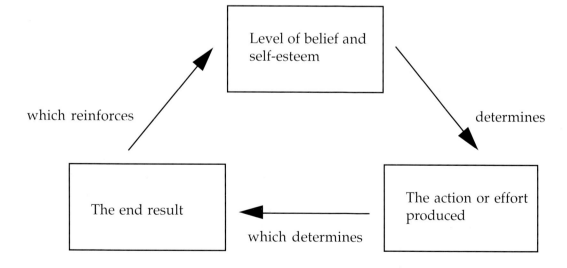

Building self-esteem Those with high self-esteem will accept greater challenges and take on tasks with far more confidence than those with low self-esteem. Success breeds success and part of your job as subject leader is to ensure that staff meet with it. This will, in turn, enable the pupils to meet with success. It is so easy to use negative language in an 'off moment' which means much more to the hearer than it does to you and has a negative impact. Telling individuals that the task you have given them is very hard and they might not manage it is inviting them to fail. You will have set up the idea with that comment that it is all right to fail. On the other hand, to offer the task with a comment about how challenging it is and how sure you are that the person will cope is to invite success.

It is important, when allocating tasks, that you equip people with what they need to be successful. People fail as often for lack of belief as a lack of ability and your job is to ensure that they have plenty of both. If in doubt, consider the following grid. In it, you check that the person given the task has the ability, the resources and the belief to accomplish it. If one column is empty, you need to rectify it.

Task	Ability	Resources	Belief
Driving a formula one racing car in a Grand Prix.	No! The person has passed a driving test but has never driven anything more powerful than a family saloon.	No! The person does not have the backing of a huge team nor the funds to buy and maintain a racing car.	Yes! The person really believes he or she could drive a racing car successfully if given the opportunity.
Developing end of unit assessment tasks for the subject.	Yes. The person knows enough about the subject and what is in each module to devise a test for each one.	Yes. The person has been given plenty of non-contact time and a small budget to buy the necessary materials.	No. The person thinks that devising these assessments is too hard as he or she has never done this sort of thing before.

With the first example, you are faced with a super-confident person who actually lacks both the ability and the resources to complete the task you have set successfully. To equip that person with the missing elements will require you to arrange lessons at a driving school for racing drivers and to secure the funding required to keep a formula one team on the road. While this might seem marginally easier than being subject leader, the budget is considerably bigger! In the second example, the person clearly has the ability to do the task and you have ensured that the resources are available. What the person needs now is self-esteem and belief. You can help to build these by giving support in the early phases of the work and the encouragement that the work has been done well.

Competence and commitment

Having motivated the staff and got them excited about the subject development plan, you will need to be aware of the competence and commitment syndrome.

Often at the start of a new project, people will have very high levels of commitment although their competence levels are fairly low. For example, in your early driving lessons you may well have been determined to pass your test after a couple of lessons because you were so keen to become mobile. However, after you crashed the gears a few times and discovered that driving was a bit more complex than you thought, your commitment might have fallen off a bit. As your competence level increases, there will often be a rapid decline in commitment levels. As subject leader, you need to be aware of this because it will be up to you to sense when this is happening to individuals as they progress through your development plan. Once you sense it, you need to offer the support those individuals need to get over the commitment drop. Help them to increase their competence levels even more so that they persevere and succeed.

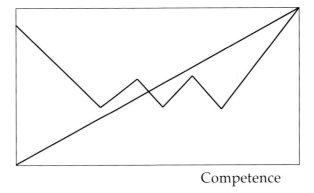

Commitment

Competence

Managing change

Implementing the subject development plan means change. If the emphasis was on maintaining things as they were, it would become a subject maintenance plan rather than a development plan. Change can be a stressful time for people and needs to be managed carefully. Managing change effectively means:
- having good reasons for changing
- involving the people in the changes
- providing training and support
- bringing in outside help where appropriate
- acknowledging and rewarding those who bring about the changes successfully.

Having undertaken the audits of your subject, you should have established good reasons for the changes you propose in the subject development plan and have shared these with the staff. There has been an emphasis throughout this book on involving all the staff responsible for the subject in the audits and the development planning process. In this way, they should appreciate the need for change and be more committed to it. The subject development plan should highlight the training and development needs of individual members of staff and how these will be met. Some of these will only be met by the use of outside expertise, people who can bring a different perspective and ensure that you are not becoming very insular.

Motivating and rewarding staff

The way in which you acknowledge and reward the staff involved in implementing the changes will depend upon how well you know them and the kind of rewards that have credibility with them. For some, this may mean a word of praise, for others you may have to resort to a box of chocolates!

Even when change is well managed, people will find it stressful and threatening. This is understandable when you consider their perspective. The top managers in the organisation have a long term strategic view of what is happening and where they are going. This is like being the captain on the bridge of the ship where you have a clear view and feel confident that you are in control. Below that level are the middle management crew who do not have the benefit of the captain's view, his telescope or his charts.

They are under pressure from above to do their particular tasks and do not really have time to admire the view. Down in the depths of the ship are the workers in the engine room making the ship move with no clear view of anything but the engines. Consequently, when asked to change, they do not appreciate why and may resist, putting pressure on the middle management who also face pressure from top management to implement the changes being demanded.

In this scenario, the captain knows that he requires changes to ensure that the ship reaches the harbour he can see but to the workforce in the bowels of the ship the reasons for the change are not visible, so resentment may result. If the captain can successfully convey the sense of excitement that he feels on sighting the harbour which makes the changes he calls for necessary, the workforce are more likely to share that excitement and embrace the changes being demanded.

It is essential to appreciate the perspective of all those involved in the subject when initiating change and to appreciate that all the staff won't necessarily share your view and excitement at the forthcoming upheaval!

The effects of change   Change will bring about benefits which is why you are embarking upon it. The only reason for having a subject plan is to improve the quality and standards within your subject. However, change invariably also means loss. This may include the loss of:

- security
- competence
- relationships
- sense of direction
- territory.

People are taken from their comfort zone during periods of change and you must make sure that they receive adequate support so that they reach the stretch zone rather than the panic one. Even change that the person has initiated, like moving house, brings the anxiety of losing the familiar, so change which is not self-initiated is likely to create even more anxiety.

Competence has already been mentioned and people need to feel challenged by the new demands on them rather than threatened. Sometimes, as a result of the changes, relationships are altered and this can be stressful. Be aware that any changes in relationships, even in the professional situation, can lead to a sense of loss.

The loss of direction can be overwhelming to some people. Those who have been lost in a city where they do not know which lane to choose at junctions and which roads to take at roundabouts will appreciate the feelings of frustration and anxiety that arise from that situation. Change at work can have a similar impact. From knowing exactly where they were going last week, people find themselves in the fast lane without a map. They are not sure that they want to go wherever it is taking them anyway! Sometimes the change means a loss of territory. People get used to their spaces and even though they may find a better one, there may be tinges of regret at leaving the familiar.

The four stages of development   You will see the subject development plan as an opportunity and have a positive view of the impact of the changes it will bring. If you have managed it well, those involved will share your enthusiasm and also recognise the opportunities. However, there may also be those who do not share that enthusiasm and they may have to go through the four stages of development before being committed to the changes. These are:

- denial
- resistance
- exploration
- commitment.

In the denial stage, people will act as though nothing has changed and carry on as they have always done. They will deny the existence of the changes, hoping that if they ignore it, it will go away and they can return to normal again. In the resistance stage, people will openly resist the change. They will at least acknowledge it if only to say that they do not want it. This can lead to anger, resentment and frustration as they try to cling on to familiar routines and habits. Beyond this stage is the exploration stage where people begin to accept that there are opportunities with the change. They begin to buzz with ideas so that concentration might become difficult because of the number of ideas they are generating. The final phase is commitment when people have worked through their frustrations and anxieties, explored the opportunities and committed themselves to the new ways of working.

To ensure that people are supported through these phases, you need to be aware of them and sensitive to how the people involved may be feeling. Keeping people involved throughout the planning and implementation stages of your subject development plan is essential to its success.

Monitoring the subject development plan

Built into the implementation of the subject development plan should be systems for monitoring its progress. This is essential to ensure that you keep to targets, timescales and budgets. If you have decided to use Gantt charts to track each aspect of your plan, and possibly the overall plan too, they can be very useful in monitoring whether you are sticking to your original deadlines. You also need to build in specific review dates when you and the staff concerned can check how things are going and whether you need to make any modifications to your plan in the light of experience.

The review dates can either be set arbitrarily, say each half term, regardless of what progress you expect to have made by then, or set for when significant interim targets should have been reached. For instance, if one of your targets includes some staff training, improved resources and revised subject guidance, you might want to review after each of these elements has been achieved. You can then check that you want to proceed with the next target in its original form.

Monitoring tasks and impact

Monitoring also takes place on two levels. Firstly, you are checking that the tasks and activities you have specified in your development plan have been carried out. That is fairly straightforward and largely requires ticks on lists. Secondly, you need to monitor the impact of these activities on the standards that pupils are achieving and on the quality of the provision. This involves activities like those you undertook during the comprehensive subject audit and these will eventually become standard practice as part of the ongoing monitoring of the subject.

To monitor the progress of the activities in your plan, you can use a simple sheet which outlines what will have been done and by when. There is an example on p. 97.

Ticklist for monitoring progress of subject development plan

Half terms	1	2	3	4	5	6	7	8	9	10	11	12
Tasks/activities												
1. Staff workshop on planning												
2. Guidance on differentiation												
3. etc.												
4.												
5.												
6.												
7.												
8.												
9.												
10.												
11.												
12.												
13.												

This kind of ticklist simply tells you that activities have been completed. It is rather like the kind that you keep to check which pupils have covered which tasks within lessons. It tells you nothing of the quality of the work done nor of its impact on standards.

In order to monitor the impact of your development plan on standards and quality, you need to build in regular opportunities to observe what is going on in classrooms, how effective teacher planning is and what is going into pupils' workbooks. This can be done either by setting up a system of checking a year group at a time or by tracking a group of pupils throughout the school.

If you choose the tracking method, you need to identify a group which represents the ability, gender and ethnic range within the school. Then each half term you would take in the books of the trackers and check what impact the activities of the subject development plan were having on the standards of their work.

Having a sample group should give you a clear indication of the impact of your development plan on the subject as a whole but you could also build in less frequent opportunities to look at whole-class sets of books on a systematic basis to ensure that the tracking group remains representative of the school as a whole. Setting up this kind of system would be an example of a task starting as a development one and progressing into a maintenance one.

Informing others of progress

You need the information that monitoring procedures can give you in order to ensure that you keep to your stated targets. Those involved in the subject also need to know how things are progressing, partly so that you can recognise their contribution and partly because the plan is not just yours. If you have done your job effectively, the plan is also theirs and they will be as keen as you are to know how well things are going. You also need to keep senior managers and governors informed of the progress of your plan so that they can maintain an overview and amend the school development plan as appropriate. Some kind of regular review sheet like the one suggested below might be useful.

Subject development plan review sheet

Date	Targets	Progress made	Impact on standards	Evidence of impact on standards
October half term	To improve planning for differentiation within lessons	Workshop held for staff which all attended	Increased understanding of the need to plan for different abilities and how to do this	Higher attainers now receiving work which stretches them and consequently achieving higher standards as shown by higher scores on weekly tests
		Guidance on planning revised to include more advice on planning for differentiation		
		Planning sheet revised to ensure teachers plan for different abilities within lessons		
		etc.		

Monitoring the budget

The other element of your subject development plan which you need to monitor is the budget that goes with it. This is important in case you find yourself in a position where elements of your development plan budget are over or underspent. In the case of an overspend, you need to be able to put your case to the senior managers for an increase in your budget. In the case of an underspend, again you may need to justify yourself to the senior managers in order to seek permission to transfer it to another element of your plan rather than to see it transferred to another subject.

In order to monitor the budget, you need a simple projected budget which you regularly check against actual expenditure. This kind of system will alert you to any impending financial crises before they hit you. You will have estimated the approximate cost of your plan when you devised it. However, some aspects might prove more or less costly than you expected. A simple spreadsheet will suffice, as your spending will also be monitored by the school bursar on a regular basis. Within your spreadsheet, you can show the targets, the activities, the projected costs of each, the actual costs when you incur them and the depreciating balance. An example is shown below.

Budget format for subject development planning

Target	Activities	Projected cost	Actual cost	Balance
Improved differentiation	Staff workshop	250	235	765
	Guidance on planning	150	150	615
	Revised planning sheet	50	50	565
	etc.			
Totals		1000		

This might well form part of your overall subject budget, in which case you might have a more complex spreadsheet with more headings. The principle remains the same, however.

This chapter has attempted to give you some guidance on how to implement and monitor your subject development plan. As implementing it has to rely on other people, there has been an emphasis on using your leadership and management skills to delegate successfully. This includes motivating your colleagues and communicating your wishes to them clearly, concisely and in a form which ensures that they share your enthusiasm for the plan. It has also attempted to raise your awareness and understanding of the nature of project management in relation to your subject plan and the way your plan inevitably means having to manage change effectively. Finally, it has offered some simple strategies for monitoring the progress of your subject development plan in terms of accomplishing the activities and of improving standards achieved by pupils.

Conclusion

Having worked through this book, you should be very familiar with the TTA national standards for subject leaders and how your own roles and responsibilities within your school compare with them. You should also be very aware of what needs to be done to ensure that you gain a clear picture of the state of your subject.

Clearly, such a comprehensive audit could not be done every year but once you have established the present state of your subject, you can implement parts of the audit procedures on an ongoing basis to monitor progress. This is the essence of effective business planning. You establish your current position and then you can see clearly where your strengths and weaknesses lie. Having established that, you can begin to plan to rectify weaknesses by using your strengths. You can also use your knowledge to influence those who hold senior management positions and have the keys to the funding you may require to improve your subject.

It is one thing knowing what you need to improve your subject but quite another getting that knowledge across to other people. If you are a naturally gifted communicator, you may have no trouble in persuading your colleagues where their strengths and weaknesses lie and what they need to do to improve. You might be able to get everything you ask for from the senior management team. However, if this is not the case, you should have picked up some tips about effective communication from this book. The most fundamental one is to see things from the other person's view, or to 'try their shoes on'. Before you can do this, of course, you have to take yours off and one of the most difficult parts of your job is to take a detached view of how your subject looks to other people, particularly those who do not share your enthusiasm for it. This is why you need the evidence of the subject audit and also the communication skills to put it across to a wide range of people.

Having got a distinct view of the state of your subject and communicated it effectively to all the relevant people, you need excellent management skills to plan and manage the developments necessary to improve your subject and raise the standards of all pupils. This means managing yourself, managing other people and managing resources including whatever budget you have succeeded in attracting to your subject. It also means distinguishing between real management tasks and the procedures and routine administration that management generates. It means avoiding the temptation to get stuck into the paperwork, which will not advance your subject but which makes you feel important, rather than into the management tasks which are essential but might not appeal.

You should have a clear idea of how to organise and run effective meetings that actually get things done and you should have cut down on those which exist only to massage egos. You should have a better idea of which of your tasks have the greatest impact upon standards in your subject and which you really should not be devoting much time to at all. You should be aiming to manage yourself and the time you have more effectively and to avoid wasting the time of other people. After all, time is expensive and you cannot go out and earn some more at the weekends to use the following week if you run out.

Unless you are a one-person subject department and you do all the planning, teaching and marking, you have to lead, motivate and inspire those around you. You might be a natural leader whom people would follow to the ends of the earth or you may need to hone your leadership skills. This book should have helped you to know where your strengths and weaknesses lie and how to improve your leadership qualities by having a clearer understanding of some of the theory of leadership. If you want to follow this up, try some of the books recommended in the reading list at the end of this book.

You cannot be an effective leader without people to lead and those people need to form an effective team. Again, you should have improved your understanding of how teams work and why some of the people in your team irritate you while others do not. You should also understand the dangers of only appointing in your own likeness and the need to create a team which has a balance across the recognised team skills. The effective leader appreciates that this will lead to conflict within the team at times but that, without that conflict, you might not be generating the most effective ideas and solutions.

This book should have shown clearly what your own professional development needs are. You might now need to consult your senior managers about the most effective ways of meeting them but you should have generated some ideas of your own. It is always more effective to go to senior management not just with the problem but also with some potential solutions. Encourage those who report to you to do that and you will be adding to their self-esteem and confidence as well as reducing your own workload. Take the same attitude towards those who are senior to you and see how appreciative they are that you have taken the initiative to identify not only the problems but also the possible solutions.

Each of us has far more potential than we ever use. Research indicates that we use only a fraction of the brain's potential, perhaps between 1% and 4%. The main barriers to accessing more of our incredible potential are self-imposed ones. They are habits, attitudes, beliefs and expectations. In looking at what your subject needs to improve it and raise standards further, always try to avoid those barriers and get other people to be aware of them too. Ask yourself and others if what you would like really is impossible or if you just have not found the way to do it yet. When I was a young teacher, there was a list circulating of reasons for avoiding change. It is a bit of fun but every time I use it, people recognise some of the items from it as being excuses they have used to avoid change in the past. Let me conclude by sharing it with you.

Reasons for avoiding change

It's been done before.
It has never been done before.
We tried something similar in 1949.
Don't they do that sort of thing in Modern Studies?
We don't have the money right now.
We are a bit short of space at present.
We don't have suitable staff.
It's a good idea but it might upset the site supervisor/cook/bursar, etc.
We would need to consult the pupils.
The parents would not like it.
I am in favour personally but the unions/inspection teams/DfEE ...
It might work in industry/FE/nursery/playschool.
It doesn't fit into the syllabus.
It's an American idea, isn't it?
It's been tried in Birmingham/Boston/Botswana.
It's not another multi-disciplinary thing, is it?
All these schemes are fine in theory but ...
The director of education would not understand it.
We are not interested in relevance; this is a school.
You've never met our School Council, have you?
Did I not read about this in *The TES/Guardian/Penthouse/Beano*?
Not if it means another committee.
Only if it means another committee.
We are awaiting the latest report from ...
Our school runs on tradition; we don't need new ideas.
I'm retiring next year but if you talk to ...
This is an educational establishment; we don't have a policy.
It might cause inter-departmental strife.
There is no space on the timetable.
It sounds too political/easy/radical/new/difficult/sensible.
You've been reading A.S.Neill/Illich/Steiner/Enid Blyton/Grange Hill.
Ah yes, but pilot schools are different.
Will it stop them writing on the toilet walls?
My staff are overworked as it is.

I hope that you will be encouraged to avoid relying on these lame excuses for evading action which might help to give your pupils a better standard of education and to implement your desired changes with confidence.

Recommended reading

Adair, John, *Effective Leadership* (Pan Books, ISBN 0330302302)
Adair, John, *Effective Time Management* (Pan Books, ISBN 0330302299)
Adair, John, *Effective Decision Making* (Pan Books, ISBN 0330287486)

Alder, Dr Harry, *NLP (Neuro Linguistic Programming*
(Piaktus, ISBN 0749914890)

Belbin, R. Meredith, *Management Teams*
(Butterworth-Heinemann, ISBN 0750602538)
Belbin, R. Meredith, *Team Roles at Work*
(Butterworth-Heinemann, ISBN 0750609257)

Berne, Eric, *Games People Play* (Penguin, ISBN 0140027688)

Blanchard, K., *Leadership and the One Minute Manager*
(Fontana/Collins, ISBN 0006370802)
Blanchard, K., *The One Minute Manager Builds High Performance Teams*
(HarperCollins, ISBN 0002550334)
Blanchard, K., *The One Minute Manager* (Fontana/Collins ISBN 0006367534)

Brown, Paul and Hackett, Fiona, *Managing Meetings*
(Fontana/Collins, ISBN 0006374077)

Carnegie, Dale, *How to Win Friends and Influence People* (Cedar, ISBN 0434111198)
Carnegie, Dale, *How to Stop Worrying and Start Living* (Cedar, ISBN 0434111309)

Handy, Charles, *The Empty Raincoat* (Hutchinson, ISBN 0091780225)

Haynes, Marion, *Effective Meeting Skills* (Kogan Page, ISBN 1850917590)

Hodgson, Phil and Hodgson, Jane, *Effective Meetings*
(Century Press, ISBN 0712698736)

Humphrey, John and Fiona, *How to Get More Done*
(Kogan Page, ISBN 0749401915)

Johnson, Spencer, *Yes or No, the Guide to Better Decision Making*
(HarperCollins, ISBN 000255027X)

Mullins, Laurie J., *Management and Organisational Behaviour*
(Pitman, ISBN 0273600397)

Nelson, Ian, *Time Management for Teachers* (Kogan Page, ISBN 0749417307)

Pease, Allan, *Body Language* (Sheldon Press, ISBN 0859694062)

Pease, Allan and Dunn, Paul, *Write Language* (Camel Publishing, ISBN 0959365834)

Pease, Allan and Garner, Alan, *Talk Language* (Simon & Schuster ISBN 0671653288)

Scott, Cynthia and Jaffe, Dennis, *Managing Organisational Change*
(Kogan Page, ISBN 0749401028)

Scott, Martin, *Time Management* (Century Business, ISBN 0712698531)

Scott, K. and Walker, A., *Making Management Work*
(Prentice Hall, ISBN 0135446937)

Useful addresses

The Teacher Training Agency
Portland House
Stag Place
London, SW1E 5TT
Telephone 0171 925 3700

OFSTED
Alexandra House
29–33 Kingsway
London, WC2B 6SE
Telephone 0171 421 6800

OFSTED Publications Centre
PO Box 6927
London, E3 3NZ
Telephone 0171 510 0180
(A catalogue listing all OFSTED publications between 1993 and 1995 is available free, reference HMI/087.)

DfEE Publications Centre
PO Box 5050
Sudbury
Suffolk, CO10 6ZQ
Telephone 0845 602 2260